DIVORCE,
THE CHURCH,
AND REMARRIAGE

by

James G. Emerson, Jr.

THE WESTMINSTER PRESS
Philadelphia

61

190

2⁵

DIVORCE, THE CHURCH, AND REMARRIAGE

*Dedicated to my parents
and my family*

CONTENTS

Preface   9

1. Introduction   11
2. The Nature of the Problem   18
3. " Realized Forgiveness " in Theology and the Bible   33
4. " Realized Forgiveness " in Pastoral Care and Church Law   49
5. The Contribution of Geneva and the Reformation Period   84
6. The Denominational Laws   109
7. The Minister's Procedure in a Meaningful Marriage   148
8. A Meaningful Law   163

Epilogue   180
Notes   183
Index   189

≪≫

PREFACE

There are at least two groups for whom a book can be written — the professionals and the large number of interested people who do not have the time or the background for wading through a heavy tome. It is for the latter group that I am writing — for the church officer, minister, and parishioner who would like to understand not only something of the church's present view of remarriage but also how that view can be improved.

This book is not a research thesis. What follows could not have been written, however, had there not first been the thorough research. Without the guidance of Seward Hiltner, James H. Nichols, and Perry LeFevre, of the University of Chicago, the dissertation that lies behind the present volume would have lacked greatly. Without the backing of the Seefurth Foundation of Chicago, its financing would have been seriously hampered. Without the cooperation of ministers, parishioners, and fellow students of family living, the study surely would never have taken place. To them all, I extend my thanks.

To the persons who have co-operated in the additional research that has made this book possible, and particularly to those officers of my own congregation who read the original manuscript, I am greatly indebted. The libraries at Chicago Theological Seminary, General Theological Seminary, Mt. Airy Theological Seminary, Princeton Theological Seminary, and Union Theological Seminary have been helpful beyond the call of duty. Since this is written for ministers and church officers, I am particularly grateful to Mr. Kendall Davis, elder at the Presbyterian Church of Forest Hills, for his careful reading of this book in its first draft.

Any author is particularly conscious of the high value of secretaries in handling the tiresome writing and rewriting of his words. Mrs. Cecil Rhodes, Mrs. Frank Gibson, Mrs. Greg Katsamas, the Misses Betty Craig, Marion Fahrner, and Patricia O'Keefe have been of great assistance in this. For the work on the final draft, my appreciation goes to Mrs. William Huck.

As with anyone who has written a book, my final thanks go to my family not only for being my most severe critics but also for patience during a summer vacation when keeping still hardly seemed a substitute for catching more flatfish or digging clams.

These words of thanks carry with them the fact that statements in this book are purely my own responsibility.

J.G.E.

1

INTRODUCTION

Several years ago in the church where I was minister, the telephone rang in the early evening. I heard the voice of an attractive woman who was active in the church. The fact that her call was further delaying an already late supper was partly forgiven by her announcement that I was to be " the first to know " her secret. She was to be married!

Such news is not exactly startling to a minister. But when the minister learns that the man in question is still married to his fourth wife, that the woman herself has seen the divorce courts, that the two have known each other only a few months, and that the marriage is to be next week, even the most casual " marrying parson " would still pause.

Yet the woman's purpose in calling was not to tell about the marriage but to say that she was going to a justice of the peace because " it will be less bothersome for you and the church." After the marriage, she continued membership in the church. When they moved to another city, with ease she transferred her membership to the church of another denomination.

This story, or one like it, could be told by many ministers, regardless of denomination. As it did for me, this kind

11

of situation has caused many ministers to stop and ponder on what this is saying about the church. What does it mean when people, with no awareness of inconsistency, do something outside the church because the church might question it, yet never question their own relationship to the church? What does it say about the church, about our society, about our procedure as ministers and church officers, about all of us?

In another church, a couple asked the board of deacons if they could be married in the sanctuary. Both the man and the woman had previous divorces. The church was temporarily without a minister. Said one of the deacons, a long-time member of the church: "What do we do in a case like this? I hear there is some sort of law about it, but I don't know what it is. We seem to have plenty of other divorced and remarried couples in our congregation."

At a meeting of one of the higher judicial bodies of my denomination (Presbyterian), a minister who knew of my interest in the subject asked me, "Just what does the church really have to say to this question of divorce and remarriage?"

Any minister in any denomination could multiply examples of the way in which this question has risen. To ministers, to church officers, and to many members of the congregations, the matter of remarriage is a real issue. No one will deny that it is a highly practical question.

The high percentage of divorce rates makes it an unavoidable question. In one source or another can be found almost any shocking statistic on the subject. Many conservative estimates put divorce rates at one in four. This means that in the average congregation, if each parent has two children, every family span from grandparent to grandchild will experience the problem of divorce and the question of remarriage. This toying with statistics can be taken too seriously, but rare is the family that has not known the pain of this issue within itself or through close friends.

Nor is this situation likely to get better. People often blame war for increased divorce rates. There is no doubt that increased divorces are a part of the wreckage of war. Nevertheless, today there are continued threats to family life that are not related to wars. There is a general heightening of tension in American life as a whole. Part of this comes from the background of international tension. Part of it comes from the speed of city life and the fact that more and more of our people are moving from the farm to the city. The aloneness of apartment living, the constant uprooting that comes with the many moves our families make, the cultural pressures of business, of social groups, and of " keeping up with the Joneses " — all these things place the family under greater tension than can be accounted for by the pressure of war.

To everyone, the remarriage of divorced people is a very practical question.

But it is not just because the issue is practical that I raise the matter of divorce and remarriage. Beneath the surface, the question of what the church should say to the remarriage of divorced people raises an even more important issue. The matter of remarriage is another way of asking, " Is the church — is the Christian faith — relevant to people where they are? "

In the area of segregation, in the sphere of management and labor tension, in the realities of war and peace, there are many persons who have wondered if the church has anything relevant to say. Some have excused themselves on the grounds that the Christian faith is basically personal and should not be involved in social issues. This excuse does

not work in the area of remarriage. The family is the basic
unit of society and the fundamental unit in any church.
Jesus speaks specifically about divorce, and Paul has many
pointed comments about family living. To avoid this issue
is to forsake the gospel as well as a personal problem.

Therefore, we must not ask merely about the attitude of
the church to remarriage. In asking it, we must also ask
if the church is relevant to people and their problems; or
if the church and its faith are just a nice pastime that is
satisfying only to some? Are a powerful gangster, a cynical
playwright, and a communist philosopher correct in brand-
ing the church and its faith as meaningless for life in the
raw?

The purpose of this book, then, is not only to see what
the law of the churches and the practice of the ministers
happen to be. The purpose is also to inquire about the
significance of the attitude. The intent is not only to suggest a new law and a meaningful procedure for ministers
and church officers. It also is to show that this procedure
is imperative because it is inherently Christian and relevant.

Jesus said that the Sabbath was made for man, not man
for the Sabbath. Since he was referring to the law of no
work on the Sabbath, we can legitimately paraphrase this
to say that law is made for man, not man for the law. In
the light of that, what of the church laws on remarriage?
Are they written for a man and a woman who have a problem, or are they imposed on the man and woman by a certain American culture to maintain the structure of our
society?

My contention is that the church laws with regard to
remarriage fit the latter category. As will be shown later,
the laws work more to maintain the *status quo* than to
speak to the needs of men and women. This statement is

true whether one speaks in relation to a couple's needs with regard to each other or with regard to God. My contention is, further, that, as such, the remarriage laws of the churches are neither Christian nor humanitarian (in the best sense), but emotional and dictatorial.

In making this accusation, the question may legitimately be asked, "What do you mean by 'the church'?" The word "church" has many meanings. It can mean the building on a corner of Main Street, a congregation, the saints who are living and dead, and so on. In this book, the use of the word is definite and clear. Here, "church" refers to the denominations. The denominations are the institutions that confront people as "the church." It is in these denominations that the institutional laws are formed and find their expression.

There are three main groups of denominations: the Roman Catholic and Orthodox Catholic, the non-Roman and non-Orthodox groups that have a strong denominational structure (e.g., Episcopalian, Methodist, Lutheran, Presbyterian), and the "free" churches (e.g., Congregational, Baptist, Society of Friends). The main emphasis will be on the second of these three. The churches in the first group have no official recognition of divorce. Hence, they can have no official view of remarriage. (Nevertheless, what is said here would also apply to cases of annulment.) Churches in the third group leave the law in the hands of each congregation. Counterparts of the attitudes of the Congregational, Baptist, and Society of Friends groups will be found in our case histories. However, it would be outside the scope of our interest to attempt a survey of each church that, despite confederate relations, is basically a law unto itself.

If the discussion in this book should seem to the reader to have a Presbyterian flavor, I plead "guilty as charged."

There is good reason for this. Anyone who would be qualified to write a book such as this would have to be related to a denomination. It would be inevitable that he would have a certain point of view. I am a Presbyterian. Further, my study initially centered on the Presbyterian Church.

This fact does not invalidate my look at this problem. Since everyone has a few prejudices, it is only those persons who will recognize them who can guard against losing their objectivity. In addition, a look at the other churches has revealed that the problem of remarriage is not basically different from denomination to denomination. The difference in church outlook puts a different expression of the problem in each denomination, but the basic emotions, feelings, and concerns are the same.

There is an additional reason why this Presbyterian prejudice is justified. One way to evaluate the present law of a church is to compare it with the law of contemporary churches and of similar churches of many years ago. Only in the Presbyterian tradition is it possible to find laws on remarriage that come from an entirely different era and culture.

The Episcopal laws can easily be traced to England from the founding of our country, but there were no detailed laws written in the time of Henry VIII. Luther had a view on remarriage, but he was far more a writer of ideas and concepts than of laws. Only in Calvin's Geneva of the sixteenth century are there real laws that can be contrasted with the laws of today. These are not just the ideas of one man but the debated and voted statutes of a particular government. For that reason, they form a perfect comparison with the debated and voted statutes of today's church governments.

Finally, this book is written out of the context of pastoral

counseling experience. Although each story has been al-
tered to prevent identification, the problems are real. Every
situation has happened at least twice in the course of my
work with families and in marriage counseling.

Thus introduced to the book, we are now prepared to
ask, "What is the nature of the problem that faces us?"

2

THE NATURE OF THE PROBLEM

In the matter of remarrying divorced people, the real question is this: What is it that makes a person ready for marriage? The church laws might be described as an attempt to state what constitutes "readiness to marry."

This question is the fundamental one in any culture or religion. In the Roman Catholic Church, marriage is considered a sacrament. Therefore, to experience this sacrament once means that an individual is not ready to marry again. Since the sacrament creates a situation called "one flesh," a person is not free to remarry unless that "one flesh" has been destroyed through death. (Even with regard to death, in many historical periods the Roman Catholic Church was rather reluctant about remarriage.)

For almost everyone in the Christian tradition, the presence of one wife or one husband prevents "readiness to marry." In America, this position was heightened by the reaction to the Mormon Church in the last century. All the traditional churches state that a person cannot marry if he has a wife. The laws are often amusingly silent on the matter of a woman having more than one husband, but I assume that women's suffrage extends to this matter too!

Those who understand the Bible literally hold that the death of a wife or husband is the only basis for remarriage. This is true not only for Roman Catholics but also for fundamentalist groups that consider the " escape clause " in Matthew a heretical insert. (This clause allows divorce for adultery.) Those who do not understand the Bible legalistically range from the ones who say that remarriage can come only when the innocent party to adultery was involved to those who are satisfied with merely a desire to remarry.

However, these arguments about how the Bible should be interpreted never touch the real facts of what happens when a minister meets a request for remarriage. The following interview, short as it is, contains all the basic elements of the remarriage issue — regardless of a particular church law.

Picture a young minister in the midst of cartons and boxes when he is told that a couple want to see him immediately at the church office. He has just moved into the area and feels quite " green." Wondering how people have found him so quickly and wishing he could see them in what " the books " describe as an ideal counseling room, he enters the office. He finds Mr. A and Miss B waiting impatiently for his arrival. After the required pleasantries and a few sparring remarks about the weather and other nonessentials, the minister says:

MINISTER: Well, I gather you'd like to get married.
MISS B: Yes. We recognize that there are certain problems, though. What's the rule when a divorce is involved?
M (*startled at the sudden discovery of a divorce involvement*): Well, uh, technically, the rule is that you can remarry the innocent party after one year has elapsed.

But that is really left to the discretion of the individual minister.

MR. A: We have the papers here. Would you like to see them?

M: Yes, thank you. (*The papers revealed that both people had been divorced. One had been divorced three times on the ground of mental cruelty, and the other had been divorced twice on the ground of desertion. The most recent divorce was only four weeks old.*) I didn't realize how recently you had been divorced.

MISS B: Well, it is recent, but we had been separated for two years.

M: I see. (*Pause.*) When would you want to get married?

MR. A and MISS B: Next week.

M: (*Pause.*) Well, I just couldn't do it that soon. In a situation like this, I would not be justified in going ahead without the approval of presbytery. It will be three weeks before they have a meeting and I can take it up with them. If it were a question of just one divorce, and if the year were almost up, I could make the decision. Here, though, my hands are really tied.

MR. A: We understand. (*Somewhat sarcastically.*) We wouldn't want anyone to go against his regulations.

M: If you wanted to wait and have me really go into this with you, I'd be glad to. But a week is just too soon.

MISS B: We'll think it over. In the meantime, thanks for your time.

The couple disappeared as quickly as they had come and were never heard from again. The question here is: What and who were involved that made this marriage impossible?

The studies in the remarriage of divorced people show

that, contrary to popular opinion, more than one or two people are party the situation. There is the minister, there is the couple, and there is the corporate body of the church. Some people act as though only the couple are involved and only they have to make a decision. Others, such as this minister, act as though only he has to make the decision. Few Protestants, particularly in the free church groups, recognize the reality of the church as a party to the decision.

In this interview, it is clear that all three were involved. The minister was involved because the couple asked him to officiate. However, the man and woman, not the minister, were the first ones who had to make a decision. Had they not come to a conclusion, the minister would never have been involved. And before they had gone very far, both the minister and the couple realized that they were face to face with a third party, the church. The church had a law. The church also had a " people " who could interpret and change that law.

Regardless of the structure of one's church, wherever there is a request for remarriage counseling, these three parties are present. If this statement seems too obvious, one need only search for a church law that does recognize all three. He will have a long search.

The " what " that was lacking in this marriage interview is the most important element in the whole discussion of the remarriage of divorced persons. It is the absence of what I have termed " realized forgiveness."

What happened in this short interview was a display of many guilt feelings. Realized forgiveness is the element that a careful study of remarriage interviews has revealed to be the most crucial.

" Realized forgiveness " may be a new term, but it is not

theological jargon. It is only the "doctrine of forgiveness" that is a theological term. Theologically, the Christian position holds that the forgiveness of God is always present. It is the Christian position that the forgiveness of God is demonstrated through the crucifixion. Yet, despite theology, many people in our churches have no sense of forgiveness. Intellectually, they know that they are forgiven, but this forgiveness for actual wrongs or failures is not real in their everyday living.

A case in point is the story of a young man from a conservative background who had fallen in love. He thought he was going to marry the girl. The more they dated, the more they engaged in petting. At times this went pretty far, but the boy justified it to himself on the ground that he was going to marry this girl. One night, they got so caught up in their emotions that they forgot everything. Said the boy, "We didn't go all the way, but it was the next thing to it."

A year later, the couple broke up. Suddenly, the man in question had all his rationalization for his actions shattered. He began to have sleepless nights; he found he could not pray; he began to develop stomach disorders. That was his situation when he came for counseling. In the course of talking with the minister, he began to explore his feelings and his actions with the girl. He felt guilty but had not been able to admit it to himself. The next day in church, he heard the minister speak not only of needing to believe that God forgives but of living as actually forgiven. Later he talked about his guilt and discovered that the minister forgave. The one who was not forgiving was he himself. The next Sunday was Communion. During the silent prayer, he confessed anew his whole feeling to God. The Sacrament he received as symbolic of the forgiveness of God. "You know," he said, "when I walked out of that place, I felt like a new man." The doctrine of forgiveness is theological. The realization of forgiveness in one's life is not a doctrinal issue; it is a personal experience.

Any remarriage interview brings with it many hidden guilts. These guilts result in tensions and barriers to a new marriage. The significance of these guilts will be discussed later. The point is that without a sense of the reality of forgiveness, so that one can say, " I feel like a new man," remarriage is impossible.

Specifically, I define realized forgiveness as the awareness of forgiveness to such a degree that a person is free from the guilt he feels. For health, this is as important as an awareness of the guilt. It is this experience that must ultimately be seen if anyone is to be ready for remarriage.

For this to happen, one must have a knowledge of his genuine guilt. Often, an interview will show that a person feels guilty for adultery. At the same time, this person may have difficulty feeling that God has forgiven him for that act. The writings of Freud and others indicate that there is more than one reason for this difficulty. The primary reason is that the real guilt is far deeper than the fact of having gone to bed with someone else's wife.

By committing adultery, the person in question may have violated his own image of what he himself is like. His real guilt may be against himself. On the other hand, there is the question of having taken liberties with another personality and betrayed a trust. The Reformers Calvin, Luther, and Zwingli all saw adultery as more than just a physical relationship. Equally, from the standpoint of psychotherapy, adultery is more than an act; it is a symbol. Before a person can be fully conscious of forgiveness, he needs to be aware of that for which he needs to feel forgiven. However, awareness of the real guilt is not enough.

I can be aware of not speaking fluent French. The greatest regret in the world for this will not help the French. I could become so involved in my regret that I could never talk with a Frenchman.

By the same measure, some people become so involved in their guilt that they are in bondage to it. In addition to knowing the guilt, one must be free from its hold. The experience of realizing forgiveness is the positive dimension that makes one free from bondage to a past guilt. Calvin's discussion of absolution clearly recognized this. The modern insights of psychotherapy recognize the importance of accepting knowledge of one's guilt.

It must not be thought, however, that these two always follow in a logical order. The sense of guilt and the sense of forgiveness can hit the person at the same time. In the presence of the love and understanding of the minister, the parishioner comes to feel loved and understood. As one person expressed it, " It suddenly struck me, as I was feeling terrible about what I had done, that if you could still accept me, why, so could I." Because he felt forgiveness on the part of the minister, he could feel forgiveness within himself.

In the interview above with Mr. A and Miss B, this need for forgiveness was evidenced by the couple and the minister. The minister felt guilty because he was not sure of himself, of how to meet the situation, and of whether or not the law he had to interpret was fair. The man and the woman both had had very recent divorces. There was no evidence anywhere of their having been aware of any sense of guilt, much less any sense of forgiveness. On the contrary, their concern for speed, their impatience with the concerns of the minister, the note of sarcasm in the statement about not going against the rules, and the fact that they did not return are evidence that they had a defensiveness about their guilt. There was no sign of trying to open up and come to terms with the whole situation.

The account of this interview is of value, then, not only because lack of forgiveness can be observed but because it can be observed in the minister as well as in the couple. If the minister felt guilty about his relationship to the situation, how could he hope to mediate forgiveness to the couple? What happened to cause this interview to fail was the inability not only of the couple but of the minister to experience real forgiveness. The pastor was so bound by his feelings of guilt that he was not free to minister to the needs of the couple. Had he been free, he would not have married them; but he might have helped them gain insight into the meaning of their situation. The whole story would then have been quite different.

In the light of this discovery, many of the popular questions about remarriage are the wrong questions. The fact is missed that statements about adultery or desertion or innocence all ultimately refer to whether or not forgiveness can be realized after a divorce.

Most ministers approach remarriage requests in the wrong way because they think of remarriage as just a legal question. There are legal matters involved in remarriage, but it is a false assumption to think that remarriage is to be treated only legalistically. One minister said it was against his principles to remarry a divorcee. A West Coast minister said that he had some scruples about the matter, but that these scruples had at no time caused him to tell a couple he would not officiate at their wedding. Most ministers are in the middle. Their attitude is reflected by the pastor of twenty years' experience who said: "I really don't know what to do; I just feel my way along. Sometimes I stand very rigidly by the rule and marry only the innocent party;

other times, the two people seem so sincere that I cannot do otherwise but marry them."

Each of these ministers is asking questions about the law and his relationship to the law. The first found his answer in doing exactly what the letter of the law said. The second rejected the law entirely. The third seemed to abide by the law usually but to violate it occasionally — and probably had a guilt complex as a result!

Yet, is this just a legal problem? In view of the statements about "realized forgiveness," the answer must be a resounding, "No!" Remarriage is not a legal problem unemotionally related to the individuals involved. The tragedy in the above three approaches is that there seems to be no awareness of the questions that are asked by the couples who come for help. The clergy, generally, seem to miss the questions being asked that are central to all remarriage issues.

Although it is not ordinarily disputed, this legalistic approach of ministers could be further documented by reference to the debates of this matter in official church assemblies. For example, in one presbytery of the Presbyterian Church, there was a twenty-minute argument about the reactivation of a committee on the remarriage of divorced persons. Every statement in this discussion was one of procedure. The entire issue was seen on a legal basis and did not raise the problem of the individual relationships involved. This was despite the fact that the discussion was begun by a plea from a minister for guidance and support in dealing with the matter of remarriage.

In view of this factor of "realized forgiveness," most laymen appear to be closer to the heart of the problem than are the clergy. However, even they miss the central issue. The following examples are typical of the statements I hear:

1. Mrs. C, a divorcee, said: "I believe that no man has the power to dissolve a marriage, no matter how badly it has gone. Only God can do this, through death. Therefore, although I am the one who went to Reno, I will not remarry."

2. Mrs. T, who had been divorced and was to remarry, said: "We don't want to put you on the spot. That is why we are getting married by a friend in the next state." (This is not unlike the couple who went to the justice of the peace because this marriage business was "bothersome.")

3. Mr. M, who had not yet received his divorce, but was getting it after five years of separation, commented, "I think it is high time the church got realistic about this business and married divorced people."

These comments cannot be taken as a unit. The reason they cannot sharpens the judgment made against the ministers. The ministers were speaking about the law. Each of these people was speaking about a live, personal situation. True, these were subjective reactions. That is the point. The subjective factors cannot be ignored if the true nature of the problem of the remarriage of divorced people is to be understood.

What did these questions say?

Mrs. C stated that only God could dissolve a marriage. The question implied by her was not how a remarriage could take place, but how a marriage could die. This is an important question. Since she was the one who got the divorce, however, she had a secret feeling of guilt. "Have I killed the marriage when only God can kill it?" Intellectually, Mrs. C's question said merely that a man should not play God. Actually, her question grew out of a need to feel God's forgiveness for her part in the divorce.

Mrs. T wanted to avoid putting the minister "on the

spot." I might suggest that she was being almost Calvinistic in wanting everything done " decently and in order "! For Mrs. T, the question seemed to be one of how to deal with society as represented by the minister. A look beneath the surface shows that she, too, had other questions. What is the relation between the church I know well and the rest of society? Is her church a part of life, or is it removed from life? The very fact that Mrs. T spoke to the minister showed that she wanted some degree of approval from the church. Otherwise, why did she go out of the way to tell him? This desire for its approval is another way of saying she wanted its forgiveness and understanding. Yet she was afraid that raising the issue would bring personal rejection. She was afraid that the forgiveness would not be there.

For Mr. M, the question seemed to be, " When will the church get wise to the facts of life? " His questions should here have been: " What are the facts of life? " " Is the death of a marriage real? " " Can one bury the past? " Mr. M had been separated for five years and was just about to get his divorce. When did the death of the marriage take place — five years ago, in the midst of the separation, or was it yet to take place?

There are many wrong questions about remarriage. There are also some right ones.

An excerpt from an interview with a couple contemplating divorce will help portray the real questions that are to be asked and that are being asked. Although this couple were not talking about remarriage, their situation was not unlike that of people who have been divorced and then remarry each other. The only difference here is that this couple never completed the legal maneuvers.

Usually the overriding concern of the minister in mar-

riage counseling is the preservation of the family. This
concern may prejudice him against divorce or remarriage.
Some psychotherapists and other counselors move the other
way. Their emphasis is more on the development of the
individual with, sometimes rightly, a contempt for custom.
Jean and Jack had been both to a psychiatrist and to a
minister. They had experienced this difference and felt
uncomfortable with it. In the first interview they said:

JEAN: We have come to you because we do not know what
   to do.
MINISTER: I see.
JEAN: I should tell you that we have both been going to a
   psychiatrist for the past year, and he has given us some
   help. But, well — oh, Jack, you explain it, you're the one
   he told it to.
JACK: Well, what Jean is referring to is the fact that
   Dr. ———— said that I needed to have more confidence
   in myself sexually. He said that I ought to play around
   a little, find out that I could handle women, and that
   then I would have more confidence in myself.

   (Unfortunately, it was not possible to reach the psychiatrist to discover what he meant by this comment, or if he
had made it at all. This type of comment is often errone-
ously attributed to psychiatrists.)

M: I gather that you felt not quite sure what to do with
   this suggestion, is that it?
JACK: Yes. Jean obviously wasn't very happy with the idea,
   and although she's the religious one, I just couldn't
   quite bring myself to do it.
M: If I may butt in here for a minute, I'd like to ask something. You say that you have been going to this psychiatrist all this time. Now you come to me. Why? Are you

wanting me to tell you whether or not the psychiatrist is right or wrong, or what?

JACK: No, the truth of the matter is this. We both had the feeling that Dr. _____ was interested in each of us as an individual, but he didn't seem to worry about our home. We need help on our feelings about each other.

These statements are taken from the first part of a long series of interviews in which the probability of divorce became very real. The fact that the divorce never took place, and the fact that any psychiatrist will know that Jack's last statement does not represent understanding of what the psychiatrist was doing, are not the point. Of interest are the questions that emerged in the first minute of the interview. They are easily missed; but they, or ones like them, are the real questions of any divorce and remarriage conversation.

Behind the psychiatrist's statements was the question, "How does a man know that he is indeed a man?" No one can lead a meaningful life if he does not know who he is and have confidence that he is what he is. The question that comes to ministers and church officers alike, then, is this: "How does the church answer the need of a man to know that he is a man?" Is this question answered by the church when it points the finger at a divorced man and says, "There is none righteous, no not one"? If the theologians are right when they say that a man is most truly a man when he is Christ's man, then we can say that the realization of God's forgiveness in Jack is one of the answers to his desire to be a man. This is true because awareness of forgiveness is a prime factor in helping a person to know who he is. Without it, a person can never be more than a guilt-ridden, emotionally blind man.

From the couple, there came another question — and it was asked directly of the church. "How are we to make sense out of what science seems to tell us and the guilt which our religious culture has imposed upon us?"

These two found themselves caught in the cross fire of fast living in a large city. They lived in a world dominated by what science had made possible. The interview later showed that they had had a puritanical religious upbringing. Their backgrounds were of the "Bible belt" farm lands. Jack and Jean had the problem of bringing together two cultures. They were asking the church for guidance as to how this could be done. They were also asking the question, "What is the family?" They did not feel that that question had been answered.

The minister, too, suggested a question which the church is asking itself. This is not a legalistic question, for it arose out of the personal experience through which he was passing in the course of the interview. So overpowering was the issue that the minister could not let Jack and Jean continue with their own concerns; he had to "butt in." The minister was asking, "What is the relation between the secular and the religious?" How do you relate what a psychiatrist says in a secular setting and what a minister says in a church setting? This question may betray a misunderstanding by the minister as to what the "secular" and the "religious" really are. Nevertheless, the question was asked.

Not all these questions are of immediate concern to us. Our purpose has been to see the real nature of the problem. In dealing with the remarriage of divorced persons, one is not dealing with a merely practical issue to be solved on merely practical or legal grounds. Rather, the issue of marriage, divorce, and remarriage has within it concerns that speak to the very heart of the church.

The question of remarriage is really the question of the relevancy of the Christian faith. The sense of meaningless-ness demonstrated by ministers in relation to the remar-riage of divorced persons calls to the question the credibility of the Christian message in the world. As Karl Heim has put it, " The church's future today depends more than ever on whether she withdraws into the ghetto and leaves the world to its fate, or whether she has the authority to continue the discussion with the world outside and to answer the questions which it puts to her." [1]

" What is it that makes a person ready for marriage? " is a real problem that the world is putting to the church at this point. " Realization of forgiveness " is the answer to that problem. The Biblical and theological foundations for understanding the application of this answer to a given instance of remarriage is the concern of the next chapter. The specific applications will then follow.

3

" REALIZED FORGIVENESS "
IN THEOLOGY AND THE BIBLE

Understanding of the remarriage problem has been clouded by many factors. There are misunderstandings as to what the Bible actually says. There are theological errors. There are great errors about pastoral work and church discipline. The concept of " realized forgiveness " has implications for each of these areas and helps to correct the errors.

There are persons who will wonder why the theological implications are mentioned first. After all, do we not all start from the Bible?

Ideally, we do start from the Bible. Ideally, we check and test all our views in the light of the Bible. Actually, however, everyone has certain assumptions that he brings to the Bible. These he tests and confirms in the course of reading the Scripture. This is not the place to give a long discourse on the Biblical theology that is in my mind. But there is an obligation to be clear about what the concept of realized forgiveness says about the assumptions that I, or anyone else, bring to the Bible. There is a further obligation to ask whether or not these assumptions are in accord with Scripture.

Theologically, the principle of realized forgiveness underscores the importance of a *Christian* view of time. Why should time be important? After all, everyone knows what time is. Yet people in different ages have had different ways of understanding time. Further, it is my observation that much of the present problem in understanding remarriage centers in a pagan view of time.

The importance of the time factor is reflected in many remarriage laws themselves. The common marriage laws, in the church, have been very specific about time. In some places, a certain amount of time has to pass before the publishing of the banns (an ecclesiastical form of announcing the engagement) and the wedding. With regard to remarriage, most laws state explicitly that one year has to have passed after the granting of the final divorce statement.

Political laws, too, have had a lot to say about time. In New York State, the marriage license is not valid until twenty-four hours have elapsed. Most states require that a person shall have lived there a certain length of time before he can marry. And on it goes. The factor of time is always present in the question of marriage. What most people do not realize is that there are unchristian as well as Christian views of time. If " realized forgiveness " is the fundamental element in readiness for marriage, then the implication of that for the concept of time must be known.

There are two general non-Christian views of time. The first of these is derived from the Greeks. It pictures time as a great circle. This circle is a trap. Hence, time is seen as a trap from which one must try to escape.

This view of time is spatial. A circle is a spatial image. Today it is reflected in the attitude of the cynics. Examples can be found in literature, art, philosophy, and everyday practical living. It has the motto: " Eat, drink, and be merry, for tomorrow we die."

The only thing that can be done, in this view of time, is to escape. The catchy songs of *South Pacific* suggest some of this. The men are in the torture and grime of war. What can they do? They escape to a magical island, Bali Ha'i.

In religion, this reaction is expressed in Christian Science. God is seen as " all in all." God's love is " all in all." There is no reality to hatred or anger that Christian Science recognizes within the marriage relationship. It is Bali Ha'i that is real, not the predicament of the man and woman on the mainland. The presence of antagonism as a reality in the relationship between two married people is an error. Says Mary Baker Eddy: " Both sexes should be loving, pure, tender, and strong. The attraction between native qualities will be perpetual only as it is pure and true, bringing sweet seasons of renewal like the returning spring." [2] Of divorce she wrote: " Separation never should take place, and it never would if both husband and wife were genuine Christian Scientists. Science inevitably lifts one's being higher in the scale of harmony and happiness." [3]

When time is seen as a trap, the only solution is escape. *South Pacific* does it with a magic island. Christian Science does it with a higher " scale of harmony and happiness." Both of these mean denying the place where one is.

Undoubtedly, most ministers would be shocked to find themselves compared to Christian Science in their practice on remarriage. Actually, these statements from *Science and Health* express the implied theology of the ministers who marry because they " need the fees " or on the ground that " love is enough."

To marry for the fees is to be cynical. It is to say that there is nothing really that can be done about the trap of life anyway; therefore, money can be the deciding factor.

To marry on the ground that the couple seemed "so sweet," "so sincere," or "so much in love" is to avoid all the issues. There *is* discord in the world. The ministerial justification for remarriage seems to be that love somehow transcends this and that the minister is therefore free to marry the couple. For this minister, differences — which may result in discord — are not seen as a part of personality that gives people an identity. Instead, he sees differences as something to be avoided by living one's life "higher in the scale."

The tragedy is that escape does not solve the trap of time. Escape only ignores the trap. If a minister says he will marry a couple regardless of divorce, he has not solved the problem of remarriage. He simply has conducted the service in spite of the problem.

Realized forgiveness and this approach to time are not consistent. Realized forgiveness is possible only when one works through the confines of the trap — only when one works through the problem, so that forgiveness can be real. If time is really a trap, then forgiveness is never possible. If the view of time as a circle is the correct view, then the only consistent procedure is never to remarry. Moreover, if the view of time as a trap is correct, then it also says that salvation is impossible.

To put this in Paul's analogy, if Christ is not risen from the dead, if Christ is just a magical person who calls us, if Christ has not really broken through the trap, then we are "of all men most miserable."

The second view of time comes from the Hebrews. Instead of time being seen as a circle that traps us, time is seen as a straight line that is endless. This is the historical view of time. It is expressed in the word *chronos,* from which comes the word " chronology." It is time seen as a series of events that move one after another.

This view of time is one of the great contributions of the Old Testament. It is an answer to the Greek view. To the Hebrews, time is not something that traps everybody, including the gods. Rather, time, in this sense, is created by God.

This view of time has been very popular in the last two centuries. Under the influence of Newton and his contributions to the knowledge of physics, this view has become attractive to scientists. It is a cause-and-effect understanding of time. What happens at five o'clock affects what happens at one minute after five. That affects what happens at two minutes after five, and so on. Some people felt that they could prove the existence of God in this way. If everything had a cause, they reasoned, then there must be a first cause. That was God. Since this seemed to be a scientific approach, it made many people feel quite comfortable.

Out of this understanding of time have grown two ways of looking at life in general and remarriage in particular. The one is fatalistic; the other is legalistic.

For the fatalist, since everything is the cause of something else, then all situations must trace back to other situations. Hence, there is no freedom, no help, and no alternative. If two people are married, the marriage grew out of past causes. This means that one minister will argue that he can marry everyone who comes along because it is in the stars. From the same base, another minister will marry no one who comes because there is nothing you can do to overcome the situation. (This, when coupled with a doctrine of the sacrament, happens in the Roman Catholic Church.)

Whereas the fatalistic approach may characterize Catholicism, the legalistic approach characterizes much of Protestantism. Since every result has a cause, the search begins for the cause that will or will not allow remarriage. In this view, nothing today can affect the situation. It is cut and dried. It is a legal matter of seeing what has or has not happened in the sequence of events in time. For those who do not accept what is in Matthew, this means that there is no basis for remarriage. There is no cause that can be found.

For most people in the legal tradition, however, there are two causes. If adultery can be found in the chronology of events, this causes the innocent party to be free to marry. If there has been desertion in the past, this causes the innocent party to be free to marry.

As with time viewed as a circle, " realized forgiveness " and this legalistic approach are incompatible. The point of " realized forgiveness " is that readiness for marriage depends on something that is in the present. The past has an effect on the present, but it is the present condition and experience of the three parties that make a couple ready for marriage. The validity of adultery and desertion as grounds for remarriage lies in the *possible* effect of these two acts on a person in the present. Experience demonstrates that just because a person has been wronged in the past does not make him ready to marry in the present. In fact, the unhappy experience may make him incapable of marriage.

Hence, " realized forgiveness " requires a view of time that accounts for more in personal experience than a mere historical sequence of events.

(This incompatibility is witnessed in both science and theology. Sub-atomic physics has exploded the idea that the chronological view of time is the most meaningful. The view of time that now grows out of modern science I would call time seen, not as a circle or a line, but as a field. For those persons who are interested, Karl Heim has written profoundly on this point.)

This is to say, then, that if the first two views of time are right, there is no legitimate basis for remarriage. There is a third, or Christian, view of time. Because this third view of time both requires a view of realized forgiveness and is required by realized forgiveness, I would argue the reverse of the traditional thinking about remarriage. Whereas the common impression is that the Christian faith is against re-marriage, I would say that only within the context of the Christian faith can remarriage be made theologically de-fensible and actually practical.

This Christian view of time is time seen not as a circle, nor as a straight line. In fact, it is not seen as any kind of line picture at all. Rather, the Christian faith under-stands time as an *experience of fulfillment* at the deepest levels of one's life.

The Bible has expressed this view with the phrase " the fulness of time." In " the fulness of time," Christ came into the world. Persons who are acquainted with the Bible will recall the instances where God is referred to as the beginning and the end, the alpha and the omega, all at once. This is a way of saying that everything that has hap-pened is caught in one " eternal moment." Time is an ex-perience of relationship, not of memory.

And this is exactly what everyone has in personal ex-perience. A man who is about to get married is not just the result of an experience that happened five minutes before the wedding march. He is the result of all the experiences of his life bearing in on him at one moment.

The Biblical word for this Christian understanding of

time is *kairos.* It does not refer to a god that is limited by the trap of time. It does not refer to Hebrew time. The God of the Old Testament speaks of creating the first, second, and on to the seventh, day. That is historical time. The Old Testament does not speak of the time in which God did his creating, for this is not human, historical time. Time, in the Christian sense, is when all of historical time becomes a part of one supreme moment. It is expressed in the idea of one day as a thousand years and a thousand years as one day. Supremely, it is expressed in the incarnation of God — that is, the revealing of all that has meaning in life in a historical moment.

The doctrine of the incarnation means that the love and forgiveness of God must become real to the experience of each person. This experience of the " fulness of time " or fulfillment in history is the Christian view of time. Hence, in marriage and remarriage, the need for the reality of personal forgiveness demands the context of a Christian view of time.

To this point, our position is this: the Christian view of time gives the theological base for the reality of forgiveness in personal experience. The reality of personal forgiveness is the prime factor in " readiness for marriage."

The full explanation of this view about time can be found elsewhere.[4] It has been briefly sketched here to (1) show to the minister and layman that there is a close relation between his practice in regard to marriage and his Christian faith; (2) show to all who interpret the church law that the present legal approach to the question of time is not only unwise but unchristian; and (3) observe for all concerned that there is a profound and meaningful relationship between the Christian faith and the question of remarriage. Divorce and remarriage, in short, have been seen on a narrow, cause-effect basis. The Christian faith, by contrast, sees divorce and remarriage in the context of forgiveness. Forgiveness is an experience of oneness with God, and that cannot be clocked.

Aside from this question of time, there are two other points on which realized forgiveness has implications for theology. One of these points concerns the fact that a marriage can die.

All church groups recognize this point. There is no church that does not allow, today, for the remarriage of a widow or a widower. The question raised by realized forgiveness is: How do you know that a marriage is dead? One obvious way is through the death of the physical body. The Roman Catholic Church holds that this is the only way a marriage can die. The danger of that argument is that it makes marriage a strictly physical matter, and this leads to a circle of contradiction. The Roman basis for not recognizing divorce is that marriage is a sacrament. This is a spiritual understanding of marriage. Hence, marriage is not just physical. If, therefore, a marriage can die, the spiritual as well as the physical part must have died. Not only that, but the physical is the evidence of the spiritual death of the marriage. How can it be held on the one hand that marriage is a spiritual sacrament which can never be broken and on the other that physical death breaks the bond? The answer that God has broken the bond by taking the person in death is not sufficient. This reply quickly runs into problems about the nature of a sacrament.

The people who have been the most consistent at this point are the Mormons. They hold to the total indissolubility of marriage. When a husband or wife dies, the marriage holds in heaven. Although I clearly do not agree with it, this view is consistent at the point where the Roman Catholic position is not.

The fact that forgiveness is the key element in remarriage implies that the death of a marriage is a spiritual matter as much as a physical one. It may be killed by physical factors, but death is only one of these. Adultery, desertion, and others may be just as real. One of the factors in helping a person realize forgiveness is to deal with the manner in which the marriage died.

The other point for which realized forgiveness has an implication is the matter of truth. If forgiveness is a real, personal, and true experience, then it cannot be legally identified only with a law. It is the Reformation position that truth is not identical with its expression. As Calvin said with regard to culture and the truth of the gospel:

> Whereas it has been a principle received in the church from the beginning, and ought to be admitted in the present day, that the servants of God should teach nothing which they have not learned from him, yet *they have had different modes* of receiving instruction from him according to the variety of periods; and the present mode differs from those which precede it.[5] (Italics mine.)

With regard to remarriage, this means that we must differentiate between the mode in which the Bible or we speak to the issue of remarriage and the command of God about remarriage. Because each person is different from every other person, the mode by which forgiveness will be expressed will never be duplicated. There is no one law, phrase, or pattern that can be laid down. All we can do is enunciate the great principles.

The question now is: Do the principles suggested really grow from and find confirmation in Scripture?

Does all that has been said fit the Biblical view? The

Bible speaks only obliquely about the remarriage of a divorced person. Those who quote the Bible as being against remarriage have jumped to a false conclusion. These people are quite right in saying that Jesus was against divorce. It is also probably correct that the escape clause of adultery was a later addition to what Jesus actually said. To argue that divorce should not be, however, is not to say that remarriage should not be. The one may logically follow the other, but the logic cannot be assumed. When two people come to be married, they are not asking, Was it all right for us to get a divorce? They are asking, Is it all right for us to get married?

Recent statements in the denominational records reflect this difference. There was a time when most reports were headed with the title " Marriage and Divorce." Today they usually are called " Marriage, Divorce, and Remarriage."

What is the Biblical view of remarriage? Forgiveness is at the heart of the gospel. The discovery that forgiveness is at the heart of the remarriage question should cause people not to make a premature judgment against remarriage. Consider the development of the Biblical position in this field.

The present-day differences in the approach to the question of remarriage can be traced back to the early rabbinical schools. Shammai, the leader of one pre-Christian school, held that a man could not lawfully divorce his wife except for actual physical, sexual immorality. This sounds strongly like the present law in some states (e.g., New York). Shammai's interpretation was literalistic. From this, it may be suspected that he operated on a legalistic basis rather than on the personal, dynamic one considered important here.

The leader of the other great rabbinical school, Hillel,

took a different approach. He interpreted the code sym-
bolically and said that a man could divorce his wife if he
found *anything* offensive in her. It is possible that Hillel's
view was extremely subjective. However, Hillel was a
scholar of great integrity. His name has been carried down
to the present day in that Jewish centers on most university campuses are called "Hillel Foundations." The evidence suggests that he had an approach that was somewhat related to the one presented here. Regardless of their
differences in approach, both men did hold to a legitimate
basis for divorce and remarriage.

Within the Old Testament, a trend is discernible. Politi-
cally, this trend might be called "women's suffrage." It
was a trend that tended to give to women a greater degree
of equality with men in the question of divorce. It also
showed a growing awareness of the nonlegal factors involved in this matter.

The basis for the Old Testament view is found in Deut.
24:1, which reads, " When a man takes a wife and marries
her, if then she finds no favor in his eyes because he has
found some indecency in her, he writes her a bill of divorce and puts it in her hand and sends her out of his
house."

Here is the legal basis for divorce. This hardly seems to
be an example of giving a woman equality. Obviously, the
power is in the husband's hand. Nothing is said about
what happens if the woman finds some "indecency" in
her husband!

Actually, this law was an advance for women. In referring to this law, Jesus said that Moses gave it for "the
hardness of your heart." The "hardness" that this rule
corrected was a practice whereby a man would simply
desert his wife, have nothing to do with her, and give no

indication that she was free. By giving her a writ of divorce, the wife then had evidence whereby she could establish her release from obligation to her husband and, thus, her freedom to marry another. The pre-Deuteronomic rules made no such provision.

In Malachi, the place of the woman in marriage is even more strongly expressed. " Have we not all one father? " asked the prophet. " Has not one God created us? "

> Why then are we faithless to one another, profaning the covenant of our fathers? Judah has been faithless, and abomination has been committed in Israel and in Jerusalem; for Judah has profaned the sanctuary of the Lord, which he loves, and has married the daughter of a foreign god. May the Lord cut off from the tents of Jacob, for the man who does this, any to witness or answer, or to bring an offering to the Lord of hosts!
> And this again you do. You cover the Lord's altar with tears, with weeping and groaning because he no longer regards the offering or accepts it with favor at your hand. You ask, "Why does he not?" Because the Lord was witness to the covenant between you and the wife of your youth, to whom you have been faithless, though she is your companion and your wife by covenant. Has not the one God made and sustained for us the spirit of life? And what does he desire? Godly offspring. So take heed to yourselves, and let none be faithless to the wife of his youth. "For I hate divorce, says the Lord the God of Israel, and covering one's garment with violence, says the Lord of hosts. So take heed to yourselves and do not be faithless." (Mal. 2:10-16.)

In the New Testament, the views on marriage and divorce are contained in sayings by Jesus and Paul. As in the Old Testament, some might argue that these two people represented different points of view. Both Jesus and Paul are opposed to divorce, but both have a concept of the death of a marriage. According to Paul, "a married woman is bound by law to her husband as long as he lives; but if her husband dies she is discharged from the law concerning the husband. Accordingly, she will be called an adulteress if she lives with another man while her husband is alive. But if her husband dies she is free from that law, and if she marries another man she is not an adulteress." (Rom. 7:2-3.)

Taken alone, this phrase could mean that adultery was seen only in a physical sense. On the other hand, Jesus said, "I say to you that every one who looks at a woman lustfully has already committed adultery with her in his heart." (Matt. 5:28.) If one wanted to twist words, it could be argued that Jesus was even more liberal than Paul at this point. If divorce was legal for adultery, and if lusting after a woman was adultery, then divorce was legal for just looking hard at a woman! Such reasoning is ridiculous; but the only way to avoid it is to assume that Jesus was not legalistic or literalistic in his understanding of adultery or marriage.

What Jesus means is further complicated, when taken literally, by the fact that whereas in Matthew, Jesus' quote allows for divorce on the basis of adultery, in Mark it does not. The Matthew reading is:

> "Have you not read that he who made them from the beginning made them male and female, and said, 'For this reason a man shall leave his father and mother and be joined to his wife, and the two shall become one'? So they are no longer two but one. What therefore God has joined together, let no man put asunder. . . . And I say to you: whoever divorces his wife, except for unchastity, and marries another, commits adultery." (Matt. 19:4-9.)

Again, in Paul, there is evidence that he too did not interpret life either legalistically or physically. After the pas-

sage where he spoke of a wife's freedom to remarry after
her husband had died, he went on to speak about death.
" Likewise, my brethren, you have died to the law through
the body of Christ, so that you may belong to another, to
him who has been raised from the dead in order that we
may bear fruit for God." (Rom. 7:4.) This statement alone
shows that he held to more than just a physical definition
of " death."

If we were to make sense out of these passages on a
literalistic or figurative basis, we would have either confusion or blindness to the facts. Only in the context of forgiveness as an experience does the New Testament attitude
toward divorce and remarriage fit together. Paul, in Ephesians, and Jesus showed that marriage to them was a corporate experience that involved the whole of existence.
Because of this, and because separation from God is sin,
and because separation from one another is a part of separation from God, Jesus hated divorce as strongly as Malachi said that God hated it. But Jesus did not stop there.
He went on to show the truly deep and personal nature
of the sin involved in immorality. For Jesus, adultery
was not just a simple, physical act. It was a deep, pervasive
factor that took in all of a person. Adultery was such a part
of all sin that even lust was adultery.

As we have seen, both Paul and Jesus recognized the
fact of *the death of a marriage*. Paul showed that a marriage could die through the death of a husband or wife.
He also said that the survivor could remarry. Since he is
very clear that one can die in more ways than just physically, what does this have to say about other means that
might cause a marriage to die?

Paul, explicitly, and Jesus, by implication, recognized
the validity of remarriage. Paul's statement on this point
has already been quoted. Jesus, when asked about the

woman who had five successive husbands, all of whom died, said that she would not have any of them in heaven. In heaven there is neither marrying nor giving in marriage. He seemed to accept the legitimacy of remarriage when a prior marriage had died. Certainly, he nowhere condemned it.

For both Jesus and Paul, marriage was not to be for some people, yet it was not to be denied others. Paul wished that all could be like him — single! Yet he said that it was better to marry than burn. Jesus likewise said: "There are eunuchs who have been so from birth, and there are eunuchs . . . for the sake of the kingdom of heaven. He who is able to receive this, let him receive it." (Matt. 19:12.) The underlying principle is the matter of personal service to God. Two marry in order to become one flesh. Another remains unmarried. In both cases, the act is done because that is a part of what one feels called to do in the presence of God.

What, then, is the New Testament view? Jesus was against divorce, and so was Paul. The actual question of remarriage after divorce is never asked or answered by either. Yet both recognized that separation did occur. Sin is in the world. To deny the effect of forgiveness in freeing a man or woman from bondage to the sin of a broken marriage can be done only in violence to the concept of forgiveness and the approach Jesus and Paul took to death, marriage, and the family itself. In short, the only statement consistent with the New Testament is to say that remarriage or celibacy depends on what one feels called to do in the presence of God.

4

"REALIZED FORGIVENESS" IN PASTORAL CARE
AND CHURCH LAW

To many who read this book, the term "pastoral theology" may be new. To others, it may not be new, but is not understood. For years, people have thought of "pastoral theology" as no more than a pretty phrase to dignify seminary courses in the practical aspects of church work. It meant nothing more or less than studying the tools of the trade. As such, it was of interest to ministers only.

Recently, thanks in large part to Seward Hiltner,[6] pastoral theology is being understood again in its proper sense. As such, it is as much the concern of the layman and church officer as of the minister.

There are a number of definitions of pastoral theology. At best, any definition must be tentative because the area is so "new" to our generation. I define it as the theology of personal relationships between two or more people in which, through the discovery of real needs, something happens to make them more or less aware of the presence of God in the situations at hand.

This definition puts church administration in a different light from that of just "practical work." It means that there is a theological dimension to the relationship of a board of trustees to its congregation. The study of this relationship is the study of what happens in the government of any church to help make God's presence real.[7]

It is at this level that we are talking when we speak of the remarriage of divorced persons. We are not concerned simply with law as law. We are not concerned simply with the "proper procedure." We are primarily asking, What helps the minister, church officer, and congregation, on one side, and the couple in question, on the other, to be aware of the ministry of God in their situation? As stated in the preceding chapter, this sense of awareness in remarriage has its root in realized forgiveness.

In remarriage, the area of pastoral theology that probably concerns church officers most is the area of law. As the representative of the denomination, law is important to the minister, but he is also concerned with counseling. The average church officer, however, is apt to face the legal aspects of the question but might never be involved in counseling.

What does "realized forgiveness" have to say about church law? On the basis of the proposition that "realized forgiveness" is the fundamental factor in remarriage, one rule follows: the law cannot be interpreted legalistically!

This statement seems strange. As one lawyer put it, "How else do you interpret a law?" Or as another said, "I thought laws were written to give a definite and stated answer."

To say that a law can be understood legalistically, and to say that it *has* to be understood that way, are two different things. In the history of law, this has been a long battle. There are those persons who have held that laws should be understood specifically as written. There are others who emphasize the "spirit" of the law. Every law must be interpreted. It is the way it is written, *and* the way it is interpreted, that determine whether or not it is legalistic. I would call a legalistic interpretation one where the concern was for the law; I would call a nonlegalistic interpretation one where the concern was for the person or society involved. Only the latter approach is consistent with " realized forgiveness."

Nor is this position without support among some of the nation's leading jurists. Said the late Justice Benjamin N. Cardozo:

> Nothing is stable. Nothing absolute. There is endless " becoming." . . . In this perpetual flux, the problem which confronts the judge is in reality a twofold one: he must first extract from the precedents the underlying principle, the *ratio decidendi;* he must then determine the path or direction along which the principle is to move and develop, if it is not to wither and die.[8]

Likewise Dean Roscoe Pound, formerly of Harvard Law School, spoke of the last century as having a negative voice of law. Law was seen merely as a technique for keeping people in line.[9] In pointing out that this view of " strict law " is but one view in the history of law, Dean Pound stated:

> I am content to think of law as a social institution to satisfy social events — the claims and demands involved in the existence of civilized society — by giving effect to as much as we may with the least sacrifice, so far as such wants may be satisfied or such claims given effect by an ordering of human conduct through politically organized society.

More than any other denomination, those who call themselves " Calvinists " are pictured as adhering to the " strict law," or the legalistic interpretation. In many instances, this picture is accurate. Church discipline has had a negative connotation just as has secular law. Church law has seemed to be a multiplication of " don'ts " and unpleasant taboos.

It is therefore surprising to discover that Calvin never had this view of the " strict law." His concern was solely that of the purity of the church. On one occasion, he even counseled that an imprudently married couple not be disciplined for the good of the church! [10] John T. McNeill, in his book on Calvinism, has rightly pointed out that the Reformer's central concern in discipline was the preservation of the integrity of the Lord's Supper. In the " Article Concerning the Organization of the Church and of Worship at Geneva," we read:

> It is certain that a church cannot be called well ordered and regulated unless in it the Holy Supper of our Lord is often celebrated, and attended — and this with such good discipline that none dare to present himself at it save holily and with singular reverence. And for this reason the discipline of excommunication, by which those who are unwilling to govern themselves lovingly, and in obedience to the Holy Word of God, may be corrected, is necessary in order to maintain the church in its integrity. . . . The principal order that is required, and of which it is appropriate to take the greatest care, is that the Holy Supper . . . be not stained and contaminated.[11]

The relationship between the view of " realized forgiveness " and the position of the Reformers will be discussed later. The point on which to be clear is that there is a dynamic basis for understanding laws. This dynamic basis has strong support in both the Reformers and modern jurists. It is the only approach that is consistent with the insights concerning " realized forgiveness."

Most church people feel that the counseling of remar-

riage requests is the concern of the minister alone. This
error is one of the facts that has led to the mess that the
churches now have concerning remarriage. Modern practice has tried to make only the minister responsible.

Consider the facts. Couples do not know the laws. Hence,
they are at the mercy of the minister for information. If they
do know the laws, it does not help much. Most laws tell of
the minister's rights, not of the couples'. For example, in
some laws, referral beyond the local pastor is possible. However, the law provides for these referrals only if the *minister*
has doubts. This is in spite of the kind of evidence shown
in the interview cited earlier that the minister is not the
only one who makes a decision.

If it means anything at all, " realized forgiveness " means
that *the care of a couple desiring to be remarried is as
much the concern of the layman as of the minister.* This
will mean the following six things:

1. *In actual practice, " realized forgiveness " means that
all three parties to a remarriage situation are under judgment and need forgiveness!*

It is obvious that the couple needs a sense of forgiveness, but why do the church and the minister need it?

Consider the church. It has a decisive part in the remarriage of divorced persons. It provides the cultural atmosphere in which *both* the minister and the couple operate.
(There are times when the couple will be more aware of
this than the minister. After I had given a lecture on divorce
and remarriage, a young man in the group asked, " That is
very interesting as an explanation of what you believe, but
what does the church believe? ")

Specifically, this culture is expressed by the church law.
The couple may not know this law. Depending on the
church, the officers, and the minister in question, the

couple will find a strict or lax understanding and application of the law. As the bearer of the culture, the church
has not always played its role effectively. Church courts
have sometimes reflected group guilt feelings about being
" too easy " where remarriage was concerned. At other
times they have reflected guilt feelings about being " behind the times." Regardless of one's views on divorce, such
approaches are not true either to law or to people. The
church must know freedom from such guilt complexes if,
as an institution, it is to provide a relevant social context
for dealing with the question of remarriage. To say that it
must be free is to say that *the denomination* needs " realized forgiveness."

Since the minister is human, his need for forgiveness
may not come as a surprise, but exactly what must be forgiven?

A study of a series of recorded interviews by one minister with one couple showed some interesting facts on this
point. At the outset of the first interview, the minister was
quite nervous. Why? He was being " watched." He was
being watched by the couple. Thanks to the " mike," he
was also being watched by his church and his society. In
the second interview, the minister was far less nervous.
In the third, he showed no nervousness at all.

What happened?

Upon several replays of the tape, it became evident that
the couple put more and more trust in the minister as they
went along. Thus, as the interviews proceeded, the *minister* gained a sense of acceptance by the couple. Also, early
in the first interview, he made a little speech about the
church laws on the subject of remarriage. Hence, when
he got to the second session, he was freed from several
tensions. He had satisfied the culture by putting the right

words " on the record." He found that he was not being threatened by the couple. He found freedom to be himself, and, in this freedom, he became a better pastor.

The experiences of this minister have much in common with the experiences of many ministers who approach the remarriage of divorced persons. The pastor of today faces not only his own fears and anxieties. He must also face those that arise from lack of clarity or consistency in his denomination's position. Many ministers feel a keen sense of responsibility in performing a marriage. It is not that they are prudish. They simply have seen so much of the seriousness of family living that they cannot help feeling a sense of awesomeness in their power to officiate at a marriage. When a divorce is involved, this feeling is heightened. With it, comes the fear of being ill-equipped to handle the responsibility.

In addition, some ministers seem to fear society. Some fear being narrow-minded. Others have anxiety that grows from not knowing what the real factors are in the problems. They do not understand them theologically, sociologically, or psychologically. In order to overcome the guilt that grows out of these fears and anxieties, the minister must have an experience of realized forgiveness.

2. *In practice, realized forgiveness means that the minister and church officers must center on the people involved as they are.* This is true simply because it is the person as he is that needs to be forgiven, not the person described in a theological " doctrine of man." Often, clergymen are like the proverbial second-year medical student who said, " I don't know what to do about your earache, but I'll be glad to remove your appendix if you'd like! " We clergymen say, " I don't know about your present problem, but I'd be glad to help you into heaven! "

In her second interview with me, Dorie, a divorced girl, had been speaking about the rush of city life and the fact that this did not give her much time to think about her own concerns. Consider part of the interview and the way the minister paid attention to her.

DORIE: It's such an important thing and such a serious thing, and it seems to me that if you can't feel certain things it's very important, because it means that you can't bring everything to the relationship, and it's sort of selfish. And then, too, by talking, I feel that when you talk to Eddie [her fiancé], you can make him understand so much better than I because, uh, well, I'm just sure you could.

MINISTER: You mean you feel that I could get across to him an awareness of what you're feeling.

D: Yes. Of course, I talked to him about it; but I care so deeply for him that every time I see this look of hurt, I care so much for him that it just freezes me, you know. And that's why I think sometimes someone else can be more responsive. It's just the way I feel. (*Pause.*) I wonder if going home will help too.

M: I didn't quite get that; you say it would help him or you?

D: Well, both of us really. I don't know. I think I'll be far more relaxed in that environment, not that it's — that it's (*pause*)— to tell the truth, I'm not sure what it is.

M: Part of the trouble is to know what is the problem.

D: That is it right there. I don't know, but probably if I hadn't been unhappily married for so long, I probably would have gotten over it sooner. I don't know. I just wonder if really I'm strong enough for it. Does that make sense?

M: Um-h'm. Is what you're saying, then, that, having been through the tension of the marriage, and now in the tension of the rush, New York, you've just never had a chance to relax? Is that it?

D: I think that you have to be, so far as your mental attitude and all is concerned, I think that has to be right . . . what I'm trying to say is that I haven't really come out of it, I don't think, yet. Well, I just don't, I think that I'm progressing marvelously well, but the thing that makes it difficult is that I — it would just kill me if anything happened to our relationship, but I can't promise him anything that I don't know myself.

(*And a few moments later.*)

M: It puts the pressure on you.

D: Oh, goodness, you don't know how much! (*Long pause.*) And what it would do to me to hurt him! And that's what I'm doing, I really am. And because of (*words lost*) and all, I recognize how important it is he feel the security of my feelings, and there's probably only one way I can do that — through marriage. You understand?

M: Um-h'm. (*Slight pause.*) In a sense this is the fear that postponing it after June will be a rejection of him; I mean, that he will take it as rejection.

D: I'm afraid that he will feel that, even though it isn't. (*Pause.*) But I feel like you do; I feel this is something that has to be worked out, that I have to get before marriage. I feel that it is important, and yet I don't fully understand it. I'm sure you can probably tell by how incoherently I talk, but, uh (*pause*) if it were about anything else, but this you have to think of very deeply. And I think, too, that a lot of my trouble is, uh, I guess that things were so unpleasant for so long that I got to the place where I actually could feel nothing, like I had a barrier around me or something, so I got to the place that he could do anything to me and, huh, you know what I mean.

M: You were just immune to anything.

D: Just numb; it was horrible. And it worried me because this isn't normal, and except for the baby, the mother I felt for my child, other than that, that was the only genuine emotion I really could put my finger on, and I've been that way for so long, you understand, which, I guess is some sort of defensive action. But through that, I feel that so much of me died, and I have to kind of regain that, you understand.

M: I see. In other words, you feel there is something of you that's got to grow again, that's got to come to life again.

D: I think that that's probably the best way to put it. And that takes time, and it takes understanding, and I can't expect Eddie to wait forever, and I don't know how long it will take. I do think I've made decided progress —(*An interruption with the phone.*) I guess that's all I know, really, to put my finger on.

There are questions that arise about this interview as an interview. Did Dorie really want to get married, or are there, here, evidences that she did not? Some girls are in love with the idea of love. The engagement gave Dorie a chance to be the center of attraction without the responsibilities of marriage. Was not the comment about rushing around merely rationalization for not facing herself? And where does realized forgiveness enter here? Dorie seems to have no sense of failure or penitence for her divorce. She feels only numb.

Or what about the minister? Why did he say the things
that he did? He did not give much advice. He did not even
seem to get the point at times. In one spot, he actually said,
" I don't quite get that."

The value of this interview does not lie in the facts revealed about the case. The value lies in that there was a
real wrestling with Dorie's problem. The minister was
wrestling with it. Dorie was wrestling with it.

On Dorie's part, note the continuous flow from one
statement to the next. The minister is there, but Dorie is not
aware of being pulled out of context at any point along the
line. Every statement following his is a deeper probing
of her concern. Note also the lack of smoothness in her
statements. In the first interview (not shown here), everything was very pat. Here, she was trying to express what
she did not understand. The starts, the stops, the errors in
grammar, and the repetitions are all evidence of real struggle on her part. Yes, much could be said about the psychological factors involved here. But the minister and the
church officers do not form a psychiatric board. It may
well be that psychiatric counseling may be indicated in
time. Here, the value is that Dorie was working.

Nor was the minister just a passive bystander. He was
trying to understand Dorie's real need, and he was trying
to help Dorie understand her real need. He could have
done lots of talking. However, how could he learn Dorie's
problem without concentrating on what she was saying?
Often the minister says, " You mean," or " You feel," or
" Is that it? " These phrases fully recognize that the minister is not the only party to the interview.

In this context, his admission that he did not get a certain point was much in order. It implied recognition that
he was human and did not understand everything. It

showed respect for her as a person. He was honest with her as she spoke.

Further, what does this interview suggest about Dorie's real needs? True, this is an excerpt from an actual interview that has been picked because it illustrates a point. Nevertheless, in one way or another, this interview could be a part of every divorcee's experience.

First, it indicated anxiety in the face of the problem. The rush around the big city may have been a convenient rationalization for not stopping to think about what hurt. The desire to have the minister talk to Eddie may have been another effort to escape having to face her problems herself. If she was going to make Eddie understand, she had to understand first. What the reason was makes little difference. There was anxiety.

Quickly, this anxiety revealed itself as fear of not being accepted. It scared her to hurt someone else. " It would kill me if anything happened to our relationship."

Secondly, the interview indicates a need to know the problem as it is. Dorie was stumbling. She was trying to get to the nature of the roadblocks in her life. The minister centered on this feeling when he said, " Part of the trouble is to know what is the problem." She replied, " That is it right there."

These two comments indicated progress. An initial part of her confusion was that she did not know why she was confused. To realize that part of her upset came from not knowing the right questions, much less the answers, was a help in itself.

Thirdly, the interview shows a deadness of some genuine feelings. As a protection against being hurt in her first marriage, Dorie built a wall around herself. This worked wonderfully at preventing the sword thrusts of a breaking marriage from cutting her soul. As with all emotional defense barriers, it worked too well. It not only prevented hate from getting in to her; it also stopped love from being expressed by her. Moreover, the barrier that can keep out hate can also keep out love. Her protection was not against just harm; her protection was against personal relationships on a meaningful level.

Fourthly, there is the discovery in these interviews that something has died. A re-creation is necessary in Dorie. Something must come alive again.

The recognition of these points is progress. At the end of this sequence, Dorie had more insight than at the beginning. They may be summed as an experience of estrangement. It is clear that part of the estrangement was from people. Unsaid, but just as real, was estrangement from God. This barrier to personal relationships is a total barrier. It concerns one's relationship to a personal God as much as a personal being.

If these are the real needs, how are they to be met? Ultimately, they are to be met by the discovery — the revelation — that someone does care, that there is not estrangement, that personal relationship is possible. As with nursing the life in the muscle of a polio patient, this process takes a long time. Nevertheless, this is the need to which the pastor is really ministering.

God loves Dorie. God has forgiven Dorie. Intellectually she and the pastor know that and are reminded of that whenever they think of Christ on the cross. Yet this love and forgiveness are not real in Dorie's experience. It is in working with Dorie on the concerns that genuinely trouble her that the minister shares this forgiveness. Only as she becomes increasingly aware of her real feelings — and aware of her acceptance by the minister despite her feelings and guilts — will forgiveness become real to her. If he does not center on her as she is, this experience of relationship with someone in spite of who she is can never be experienced. This is why realized forgiveness demands centering on the person as he is.

3. *In practice, realized forgiveness means that the minister and the church officers must have real communication with the couple involved.* This statement refers to the face-to-face conversation that takes place. Often there is much talk, but nothing is communicated.

Emotionally, the reality of communication may be felt by the people as a deepening of rapport. There may also be a sense of fulfillment experienced by the group as a whole. In the context of a discussion among the minister, church officers, and the couple, for example, something may break in upon them as a revelation. It is recognized by all of them, and they know that something has grasped them.

Ideally, this moment of fulfillment has its greatest sense of communication in the service of worship. There, the congregation, the minister, and the couple would find the symbols of worship as really expressing for them the fulfillment that was taking place. Actually, though, this fulfillment gets expressed before and after the service as well as during it.

The importance of rapport can be seen in any interview. In the case mentioned earlier about the new minister, for example, the pastor did not marry the couple because he felt no sense of rapport with them. The reason lay in his own personal emotions. The minister was right in not conducting the marriage, for there was no evidence of realized forgiveness. In that interview, there could be no forgiveness simply because there was no rapport. In the interview given a moment ago, however, there was great rapport and some basic communication.

As a matter of practice, the " no " of the minister to a remarriage situation usually comes at the point of the first inquiry. In that phone call or office visit, the minister states his requirements. He says that he insists on an interview, or a look at the license, or whatever it is. It is at this instance, particularly on the telephone, that most people stop. They are not prepared to meet the stipulation of a conference with the minister. There is then no rapport, and the minister says " no."

At this juncture, the concept of " realized forgiveness " forces us to depart from a clause in many church laws. In the interest of comity (i.e., official recognition of the rights of another church in a certain area) some laws do not allow remarriage if the people have been denied marriage in other churches. Out of respect for a fellow minister, some pastors will not remarry a person who has been turned down by another clergyman.

This view is not sound. Lack of communication does not necessarily mean that the couple should not be married. It does mean, however, that the couple should not be married *by that minister*. The logic is as follows: Because any marriage discussion is a personal experience, and because a minister's feelings are a part of this experience, it is not wrong for a minister to base a negative decision on lack of rapport. To say that there is no rapport is to say that the basic condition is lacking for the experience of realized forgiveness. The failing may lie in the minister as much as in the couple, but it must be recognized as a fact. Yet if the failing is in the minister, why should the couple be penalized?

By way of example, I recall a pastor's experience with

an attractive couple that called one day. The man looked amazingly like the minister's father, who had been a very authoritarian person. The interview went fairly well and both the people were pleased at the prospect of counseling. When the day came to meet the man, a Mr. Wellington, the minister was delayed by an emergency hospital call. Upon his arrival thirty minutes late, Mr. Wellington said:

WELLINGTON: It's a little late.

MINISTER: I'm very sorry — I was on an emergency hospital call and got detained.

W: Sure, but I've got an appointment in another hour; it's no good to have a man sitting like this (*obviously quite irritated*).

M: Well, what the devil do you expect me to do? These things happen. Do you want to talk or don't you?

W (*calming down a bit*): I don't see the point of it now. How about tomorrow?

M: All right, we'll make it the same time.

In this interview, Mr. Wellington clearly had a point. No one feels comfortable about sitting any length of time in a waiting room. The minister, regardless of how one might justify the tardiness, completely missed Mr. Wellington's feelings. Instead, he became almost belligerent. Understandably, in the interview the next day, there was little rapport.

In the recognition of the situation, the second interview concluded as follows:

M: Mr. Wellington, I've come to a decision which I must explain to you. I do not feel that I can marry you. Frankly, I would suggest that you see another minister.

This is nothing personal; it is just that I have to be frank about it.

W: If that is the way you feel, all right; but why, when we've gotten started?

M: This is really rather hard to explain. Sometimes in counseling you just get a feeling that you are not able to do any good in the situation — can't quite seem to get hold of it and that someone else could. I'd be glad to suggest someone else. This does not say you should or should not get married. It just rules me out — sort of like a judge disqualifying himself from a court. Do you see what I mean?

W: Well, if you feel you can't do it, I guess so. But, uh, well, do you have someone to suggest?

From the tone of Mr. Wellington's comments, it appears that he was far more satisfied with the interview than the minister. Yet, in this face-to-face situation, the minister had his feelings. Lack of rapport and the way he felt were evidence of no communication. If the minister could not "hear" what Mr. Wellington was really saying, how could he meet him as he really was?

For the *couple*, too, this matter of rapport, as expressing communication, is important in experiencing "realized forgiveness." Both individuals come to the minister from separate backgrounds. They want to move into a relationship which the Bible calls "one flesh." I describe it as being something of an "interpersonal person." Two become one, and yet they are still individuals. There must be a point when this experience becomes real. In a church marriage, the minister is the common ground for both the man and the woman in terms of which this experience takes place.

The threats to this rapport that will allow for the experience of fulfillment may arise from several sources. There is the fact that uneasiness grows from basic lack of information. The couple simply do not know the procedure. In this regard, the minister constitutes the first real threat to their decision to marry. The couple have made the initial decision. They must then face a man whose personal views they do not know. They must face a church whose laws may be unfamiliar.

Further, the sense of uneasiness also grows from the fact that, in the minister, the couple are faced either with high subjectivity or with reality. The highly subjective minister, who has absorbed certain mores of the culture, which seem generally critical of divorce, is a threat for that very reason. The " no " of a minister, categorically stated, is a threat to the determination to marry.

On the other hand, the minister who categorically says " yes " is equally threatening. I have no records of such interviews, but such an instance would leave a couple with a feeling that they had not been confronted by something essential. Lack of awareness that they have come face to face with the minister can be as frustrating as feeling that the minister has subjectively turned them down. Both suggest failure of a real interpersonal relationship, which is part of any true communication.

Midway between these two extremes is the accepting minister who helps the couple to think through or re-think feelings. Clarifying the implications of their statements is one way of helping two people see the real feelings that they have. It also helps them to understand the minister.

In the course of the discussion, doubts may emerge. Particularly at the outset, the awareness of doubts can be very threatening to a couple. It is never pleasant to break up. The mere presence of that possibility brings apprehension. Nevertheless, working through this problem is the road to realizing forgiveness. A couple cannot do this without rapport.

The need for rapport is increased by the constant changes in the cultural situation. There is a culture of the church. There is a culture of the families involved. There is the culture of society at large. Within the course of a day, the individuals to be married may move in and out of all three. In reaction to these changes, the couple may react completely against the church. Others may give in to the church completely. Happily, some will do neither but will work through their feelings to an understanding of what is involved. As one woman said: " You know, I've had some pretty deep sores, and I've had some criticism. But now, I think I know what life really is, and I think I can bring to him real love." She had come to see her experience as a real part of her, and as something that enriched the present and prepared for the future.

The most important part of the cultural framework in which the couple and minister both stand is the denomination. This framework clearly affects the minister. He is part of the system. He has been trained in it, ordained by it, and continually made aware of it by operating as a Presbyterian, Methodist, Episcopal, Congregational, Catholic, etc., minister.

By contrast, the couple find this culture quite strange. Even if they have been active members of the church, the view of the church on remarriage will be new to them. Few have known this view other than to feel that its mood was against remarriage. Those who have known it find it strange because the view has changed in the course of recent history.

Therefore, to have a sense of real fulfillment, there must

be more than communication between the minister and the couple or the man and the woman. There must also be concrete recognition of the communication between the couple and the denomination. This is to say that rapport between minister and couple must become rapport between church and couple.

This broader rapport may be expressed partly by the relationship of the couple with the minister. It can find its most concrete expression, however, through the church officers. Some churches have a small manual on marriage prepared by the officers. Others emphasize the presence of church members at the wedding. Some churches do nothing, but most require that every marriage become a part of the official proceedings of the church. With the exception of doing nothing, all these are indications of the relationship between the couple and the denomination. The importance of this concrete relationship to the denomination is not a matter of prudishness or of distrust. It is a matter of realizing that culture is a part of our living. No life can be successful that does not adequately take into account its culture.

In standing before the minister at the marriage service, the couple stand in the presence of the whole church. The sense of forgiveness is meaningless if the couple take this stand with no awareness of what this means in relationship to the denomination. Perhaps a couple may experience forgiveness by rejecting the institutional church as outmoded but never by ignoring it.

This concrete relationship is equally important to the minister. One of his functions is to serve as the mediator between the Christian community and the couple. The danger of an individualistic approach is that this sense of community is lost. When this awareness is lost, the minister suddenly finds himself a little god. He usually becomes uneasy and insecure.

4. *In practice, realized forgiveness also means that the couple must have a sense of personal self-awareness.* We have already said that the individuals must be met as they are. But who are they? The minister does not know. Usually, they do not know either. They want to get married, but they have little real awareness of who the two people are that they are trying to bring together. They want to be forgiven and accepted, but there is little recognition of what the real failings are that need forgiveness.

It is in this area of self-awareness that the realization of forgiveness has its most profound effect. Here, each person brings together his feelings and experiences in the present moment. Self-awareness refers to the areas that psychotherapists speak of as the depths of personality.

Some may argue that only a forgiven person can be fully aware of himself. Hence, it is going in circles to say that couples must have a self-awareness in order to feel forgiven. This argument grows out of false assumptions. Actually, one does not come before the other. When a person looks at both his guilt and the fact that someone loves him, there comes a moment when he is able to accept the reality of both. At that moment, he is most fully aware of himself. Without awareness of both his problem *and* his forgiveness there is no *realized* forgiveness.

Because each person has different experiences of which he must be aware, the actual form of this self-awareness cannot be defined. Since the minister is not a psychoanalyst and the church board is not conducting group therapy, there is no basis for a psychological definition either. Nevertheless, the reality of these hidden experiences cannot be denied. Self-awareness is the ability to know oneself and one's problems as they are. This gives freedom. It may not give freedom from the problem itself, but it does give freedom to decide what to do in the light of the problem. The interviews with Eddie and Dorie are a case in point.

After several interviews with Eddie and Dorie, there was a lapse of time while the minister was away on business. When he returned, Eddie stopped at the manse to talk for "just a minute." As the conversation progressed, he said, "We have decided not to get married." He then continued:

E: There isn't very much to talk about. It was my decision and it grew out of our having more time to talk together when things weren't so rushed. I had an opportunity just to see her.

M: I see.

E: Frankly, I was just amazed when I saw her with her folks, my folks, and her kid sister. She just really didn't seem to care for anybody and was terribly wrapped up in herself. She wants a career, and that's it. So, I decided that if that were the case, she'd never really work through to a point where she could love me, or provide a real home, and that it was much better to drop the whole thing than marry under those circumstances. So, that's what happened.

As suggested by this excerpt, the interviews with Dorie and Eddie did not solve the basic problems. Even though Dorie made progress in her second interview with the minister, matters did not get worked through. Yet the interviews did help all parties gain greater self-awareness. Eddie, who started as the one absolutely sure about this marriage, came to see the problems as realities. Whether

or not he did the right thing is not the point. The lesson
is that in seeing the problems, he became free to deal with
them. In his freedom, he said, " No."

Yet anyone who has faced couples who wish to be married may well ask, " How do you know that this feeling of
freedom and this feeling of forgiveness is not just some
superficial sense of well-being? " This is the question each
church officer and minister needs to ask himself again and
again. There is great temptation to be satisfied with evidence of " good spirit " on the part of everyone concerned.
With the work load of the average pastor, and with the
agenda of the average board meeting, the task of genuine
guidance and counseling can be terribly burdensome.
There are certain testing instruments that could help. However, few ministers have the training to handle them properly, and often they are very wooden. There is, however,
in the normal course of conversation, something that can
be done.

A survey of interviews has revealed that there are some
touchstone areas which naturally develop in the course of
an interview and which can give both minister and couple
a guide. These include attitudes toward sex, family, children, and past experiences. Generally, the attitude is one
of guilt. The question to be ascertained is the place of this
guilt in the life of the person. Is he bound by it? Then he
is hardly free to marry. Has he realized forgiveness for it?
In the course of counseling with him, does he come to
feel forgiven for it? " Yes " to these questions would indicate that the person is emotionally free to marry.

With regard to past experiences, overconfidence can be
a danger sign. " The other marriage was wrong; this is
right." That statement paints a black-and-white picture
that suggests a very protective attitude. The Reformed

faith may sometimes have overworked it, but there is real truth in the statement, " There is none righteous, no, not one " — particularly where a divorce has been involved. Overconfidence prevents looking at the factors that did not allow the previous marriage to work. It defends against the hurts and the guilts. As a result, the sores never are brought to a place where they can heal.

At the end of an interview, however, a person may say: " I have the feeling that the other was just all wrong. We were too young; we came from radically different backgrounds; we were lonely. Here, the basis is different, and I feel it is right." Such a comment, which grows out of awareness of the past, is much in order. The overconfidence to which I refer usually comes at the beginning of an interview.

The opposite reaction to overconfidence is overnervousness. " I've been hurt before and I'm scared I'll be hurt again," expresses this mood. In the excerpt from the interview with Dorie this was seen. Although the phrase may suggest awareness of the past, it shows that the past has not been adequately handled. The person is still bound to it and is not free to go into something else.

The attitude toward children of divorce is also a guide. Children are incontrovertible reminders of the previous marriage. They carry to the new situation their own fears and insecurities. The new husband or wife may find them a threat. On the other hand, as in one interview, they may actually be a means of experiencing forgiveness. The following is from an interview with a girl whose fiancé had been divorced five years:

M: You say you met his son?
J: Yes. I'm very glad I did.

M: It was a good experience?

J: You can't imagine how much. I was really apprehensive. I didn't know what to expect. Somehow, when I met him, I discovered he was as concerned about my feeling for him as I was about his.

M: I see. This became an equalizer.

J: Well, yes. If you want to call it that. Somehow, it gave us a base from which to start. We've been on picnics or just around the house. And then, about a month ago, he said, " Why are you and Dad waiting so long to get married? " He is seven, and we were really able to talk about it.

Miss J had never been married. She recognized certain fears about her fiancé's child. She had taken the time to face them. In so doing, both she and the boy were becoming increasingly aware of each other and finding freedom to deal successfully with their relationship. Had there been hostility or a mere nonchalant attitude on the part of Miss J, the minister would have suspected lack of self-awareness in an important area.

The area of sex is also highly significant. Sexual intercourse is a physical act. It is an extremely intimate act. As such, it is very important as a symbol of love. The act of intercourse symbolizes the thought of complete trust. It is a way of saying, " Here, I stand before you naked, with nothing hid." To be that open with anyone takes faith. It takes even more faith if one has been married before. In the breakup of a marriage, there almost always seem to be incidents of sexual intercourse used either to prove love, recapture love, or meet a demand. As several women have expressed it, " In those last days, I discovered the beast in man." As a result of these experiences, there may be either terror or hatred of sexual intercourse. Self-awareness of these feelings is needed for dealing with them.

The effect upon a second marriage of previous sex experience is described by one person who had an extremely happy and successful second marriage. This woman originally married at an early age. At the end of this marriage, she "swore off men." Sex had become a beastly thing in her experience. Several years later, she met the person who was to be her second husband. In the process of the courtship, she fully explained her feelings and her fears. He did his best to understand and accept them. On that basis, the minister agreed to their marriage. Although they expressed their love in many ways for the first six months, they never had a full sexual relationship. In the presence of the trust and love of the husband, the experience of physical contact again became a deep and meaningful symbol of the one-flesh relationship. After the six months, this symbol could be fully appreciated by both the husband and the wife. This couple showed that they were free in relation to sex. They had a problem and faced it. In view of this freedom, the minister married them and the marriage succeeded.

Whether or not it is in the area of sex or fear, there is always *some expression of guilt*. The couple may feel guilt in the presence of the minister or the culture. They may feel a deep inward sense of guilt based on personal failure. It is to this that Presbyterian law speaks when it refers to "due penitence for past failures." A sense of guilt is not enough. It is the attitude to the past failure and the personally constructive dealing with the past failure that is important. This is why realized forgiveness calls for self-awareness.

It must be awareness not only of the past sin and failure. It must also be awareness of the forgiveness.

5. *Realized forgiveness, in practice, means not only an experience of personal self-awareness, but also of cultural self-awareness*. In the matter of personal self-awareness, forgiveness was realized in recognition of the experiences of life as they bore upon the person within. Here, forgiveness becomes realized by self-awareness with regard to the history of one's culture. When a couple come face to face with a minister, both people face two cultures. There is the cultural history of the individual. There is the cultural history of the church. The history of the church reaches its culmination in the structure of the particular day.

Today, the cultural framework that is portrayed by history is marked by a fluid and inconsistent culture. For example, the minister knows realistically that there is no such thing as an innocent party in divorce. Still, his church law points to Scripture in such a way as to maintain ambiguity about the innocent party factor. Realistically, he knows that adultery is but a symbol of an inner problem and not the real factor in divorce. Legally, he finds that some states (e.g., New York) do not grant divorce unless adultery is proven, whereas in other states (e.g., Pennsylvania) physical adultery has nothing to do with it. Therefore, in addition to the tension felt by the couple in facing the minister, there is the tension between structure and lack of structure in the church and state laws. As a common ground, the minister or church board must become the means by which this tension is sustained as the problems are met.

The fluidity of the culture is suggested by the change of couples from one culture to another, by the changes within a culture as different groups of people move in and out of a given area, and by those changes which come through the evolutionary development of any culture.

In meeting this problem, any but the Christian view of

time is unrealistic. The minister is dealing with a mass of past events all of which center on the moment at hand. He is not dealing with a series of chain-reaction events the last of which has placed the couple in his office. What happened five years ago is as much of the present experience as what happened when the couple met the secretary five minutes ago. Just because a certain amount of time has passed does not mean that the divorcee is ready for remarriage.

In the context of the Christian faith, it is the task of the minister to reject the legalistic approach about what has happened in the course of a person's history and to look for signs of realized forgiveness within that history. This is another way of saying that the minister and the couple must find God speaking in their experience as much as he spoke in the life of Christ. Practically, for experiencing realized forgiveness, this means that the past must be seen as dead. (This parallels what was said about a person's being free in relation to his guilt.)

People seem to meet the problems of culture and the desire for fulfillment either by trying to escape the past or by being forever bound to it. Mrs. G is an example of one who tried to escape. She had been widowed three times. "I have really had to deal with fear," she said. Her story showed that she had tried to escape the past by condemning it. It was bad, and she would have nothing to do with it. However, when she wanted to get married, she discovered that her attitudes to the past influenced her attitudes in the present. This crippled her effort for a marriage relationship. Only after she had overcome this means of escape and thought it through could she say, "Now I feel fine."

An example of being bound to the past is found in a Mrs.

H. She had been divorced eight years. As an attractive and pleasant woman she had many suitors. About marriage she said: " I don't know if I'll ever remarry. That experience has completely shaken my confidence in the ultimate trustworthiness of any man." Mrs. H always went back to " that experience." She never clarified it to herself. The fact that she also indulged in extramarital relations and had some definite attitudes about that practice suggested that the problem was more lack of confidence in herself than in a man. Nevertheless, the lack of confidence was directly related to the first marriage. She was not free in relation to it and therefore was bound. Hence, escape from the past, or being bound to it, may equally be evidence of lack of realized forgiveness.

Neither of these two approaches, then, is satisfactory. The minister must help the couple to see the past as past. Particularly if the woman has been the one who has received the divorce, dealing with the past is not easy. Often, men seem to have gained a sharper awareness at this point than women. In either case, however, proper dealing with the past as dead can lead to fulfillment. It is much like working with the problem of grief as described by Liebmann and others in dealing with death. It is a need to absorb the feelings and emotions of the past in a way that they can be adequately dealt with in the present.

In order to have awareness of one's personal culture and the church culture, three things are needed. The minister must help portray the church culture and the social culture so that they can be seen. He must be the common ground in the presence of which these cultures can be met. The couple must be able to bury the past and experience fulfillment in the present.

6. *Finally, in practice, realized forgiveness requires faith*

on the part of all concerned that a real revelation has taken place. Ultimately, realized forgiveness is present when a person is able to feel a sense of integrity with regard to his past and his present, his God and his culture. It comes when, within the historical progress of time, he experiences the " fulness of time " to which the Christian faith refers. This is not a matter of rapport. It is not a matter of self-awareness. It is a matter of faith.

It is a matter of faith because the decision is outside the area of logical proof. There is no test that will guarantee readiness to marry. This is not to say that the decision is irrational. On the contrary, deep thought will have gone into the validity of the marriage. However, assuming that, from an intellectual standpoint, there is every objective basis for moving ahead with marriage, one final point is lacking. There must be the personal subjective experience of commitment.

This fact is often missed in the romantic view of American marriage. Thanks in part to Hollywood, love is considered the fundamental ingredient in marriage. Love, in the romantic sense, is emotional. Love, in the romantic sense, has not been the essential ingredient in all marriages throughout history. We must remember that the arranged marriages of Europe — which make most Americans shudder — still were Christian marriages. Even today, the vows do not ask if the man and woman love each other. They ask for a promise to love. Commitment is the required experience. The theologian Paul Tillich has shown how commitment is at the center of faith. Faith is not, as popularly thought, something that enters when reason exists. Commitment uses reason, but it is not reason — it is decision. Faith is betting one's life on something.

This is exactly what happens in all marriages. It is particularly true in remarriage. There are moments of doubt

— as any prospective bride and groom will verify. There is the memory of other weddings that turned into failures — as any minister of experience can remind us. It may be that everybody is being fooled. It may be that the forgiveness is not real, that the couple are not ready for marriage. As humans, every one of us may be wrong. Yet, as with Martin Luther, there come those moments again and again where one must say, " Here I stand."

To be real, forgiveness requires, *on the part of the couple,* the courage to believe they are forgiven (in spite of their doubts). It requires the courage to commit themselves to each other on the basis of the experience that has broken in on them (in spite of the danger that they may misuse this experience).

To be real, forgiveness requires, *on the part of the minister,* the courage to believe that the revelation of forgiveness and the readiness for marriage are real. It requires the courage to commit himself to this marriage in spite of statistics, past failures, and present inadequacies.

To be real, forgiveness requires, *on the part of the church,* the courage to accept this couple as one flesh. This acceptance is shown through real participation in the marriage, through the official means of approval and recognition, and through acceptance of them as a family into the life of the congregation.

In the context of the other five points, it should be clear that this is not a pious set of statements. It should be clear that faith does not mean acting in spite of ignorance about the couple or the situation. It does not give an excuse for irresponsibility and an easy, " It's all in the hands of God " attitude. Nevertheless, the fact that many do have a superficial understanding of faith should not blind us to faith's rightful and profound place.

This commitment or faith that a revelation of forgiveness has taken place brings to focus the importance of the Christian use and understanding of time in remarriage.

Time, as used day by day, is a human invention and serves a human purpose. It is one of the ways in which we order our lives. It is, to say the least, extremely helpful in getting people to the wedding all at once. It is the basis on which the three parties to the interview are able to arrange their meeting. Everyone can agree on a certain time.

However, when this human invention begins to run our lives instead of helping us arrange our lives, the Christian is really guilty of setting up a false god. To limit one's view of time to the clock is to try to force life into a mold that does not fit. A very " scientific " college freshman advised his friends that he was going to get his education and then fall in love after graduation! He was more than a little surprised when he discovered that, somehow, the feeling of love has a way of shattering any time schedule — including a college one.

Therefore, the Christian view of time means that the minister will use the usual view of time only as a tool and as an indication that he is human. At the same instant, he will also look for the revelation and expression of fulfillment within time — the fullness of time — whenever it appears. Faith means that he will recognize it whenever it hits and not restrict it to some limit of the human calendar.

In addition, the minister must help to interpret this to the couple. He does this not by explaining theologically what is happening. That would merely provide an interesting intellectual exercise. Rather, he interprets it by helping the couple find the symbols that make the experience of the " fulness of time " real and meaningful. The purpose of the symbol of absolution in church liturgy — or what-

ever is used to signify one's being forgiven and accepted
again to the Lord's Supper — is to help the couple bring
into full awareness the face of forgiveness. The purpose of
the symbol of the marriage service is to bring into full
awareness that which follows realized forgiveness, viz.,
the fact of the new interpersonal person, the new creation,
the one flesh.

In the usual view of time, no one can control the number of hours or days this will take. Sometimes a couple
will feel ready in the midst of the interviews or, conceiv-
ably, upon the outset of meeting with the minister. On the
other hand, the real self-awareness, expressed before, may
be experienced sometime after the interview.

One engaged couple came to me after having listened
to a series of lectures on the Christian faith and marriage.
The young man had a deep emotional involvement with
his mother. He was only vaguely aware of the nature of
this involvement. His fiancée was bothered by it, but confused as to its meaning for her and their possible marriage.
As a result, they asked for a conference that extended
into several interviews. Both people gained significant insight into their problems as they talked. The last interview
ended with the man saying, "You know, a lot of things
have been clarified, but now I've more to think about." His
fiancée added: " Yes, I think the issues are pretty clear; but
we need to decide what we will do about them. That takes
time."

Throughout the interview, a degree of insight had been
gained. Yet it was only a beginning. After a period of a
few months, the couple again came to the minister. The
mother problem had ruined the young man's first marriage.
The interviews had helped him gain insight into the reasons why. The few months allowed these new insights to

become a part of him. When the couple returned, they felt ready.

As the minister, I then had to decide whether I would perform the ceremony. Because there seemed to be a real self-awareness on the part of both the young man and the woman, bcause there was a definite rapport, and because of their own testimony, I felt that the forgiveness was real in the life of these two. Yet this could not be proven. It took faith to trust this testimony. Without it, there would have been no ability to believe that these two were really capable of experiencing the work of the Holy Spirit; it would not have been possible to accept either the couple or the fact of this experience.

In concluding this section on the factors that are required, in practice, if forgiveness is to be real, an added word is in order about fulfillment or completion. The sense of the " fulness of time " does not necessarily mean marriage. It does mean that the relation of the couple with the minister, and the man and woman with each other, comes to a climax. Where the couple are sure, there is a sharpening of their reasons and their desires for marriage. The decision they made to get married before seeing the minister is re-established at a new level. They become even more sure than before, and the marriage takes place.

For others, the centering down results in awareness of what is wrong and in eventual breakup. The breakup is the climax of this latter experience. It may be the break between the two people who form the couple. It may be the break between the couple and the minister. Moving to a marriage or moving to a break, however, may both result from the " revelation " or the experience of the " fulness of time."

This point is clear if it is remembered that the funda-

mental question we are asking is: What makes for readiness to marry? The presence of realized forgiveness is not
identical with readiness to marry. The revelation, in the fullness of time, of the reality of forgiveness creates the situation in which the decision can legitimately be made. The
decision may be to marry. The decision may be not to
marry. In either case, something has happened. Eddie, referred to above, was a new person for his experience even
though there was not a new creation of one flesh.

Before we turn to the matter of the actual remarriage
in the light of realized forgiveness, let us take time to look
at the churches themselves. How did the institutional
church at the time of the Reformation deal with remarriage? How does the institutional church of today deal
with it? What is the significance of these two periods?

5

THE CONTRIBUTION OF GENEVA
AND THE REFORMATION PERIOD

The contribution of the Reformation period to our understanding of remarriage lies in its awareness of the church. I call this the corporate dimension of life.

It has already been mentioned that the tendency is to think that the remarriage decision is up to the minister. This is a day in which people think individualistically. American individualism and religious pietism have gone hand in hand. They have had a great and significant influence in the development of this nation. Unfortunately, with it has also grown forgetfulness that, as John Donne put it, "no man is an Iland, intire of it selfe." [12]

No one can live in isolation. There is a corporate or community dimension to life that is as essential and important as the individual dimension. Modern psychotherapy has come to put this in scientifically vivid terms. Long before the twentieth century, however, the people of the Reformation had put it in theologically vivid terms. In our day, people are more familiar with the language of psychology than that of theology. Although unfamiliar, the fact that today's churches grow out of a past that was aware of this corporate dimension makes it important to look at this contribution.

Luther is thought of as the first great Reformer. For the purpose of understanding the remarriage of divorced people, however, the place to start is not with any one man, but with a body of law. The law of 1560 can be compared directly with the law of today. With that law as background, then, the systematic view of Calvin and the position of Luther can be seen.

The law that best fits our purpose is the law at Geneva. It is true that this law was greatly influenced by Calvin. Beyond that, the law was also the product of a council. It is not one man's law but was subjected to debate and ratification. As such, it had great influence not only on the people of Switzerland but on many beyond the border. The general influence of this law, through John Knox, in Scotland, is known to many. What is not so well known is that Calvin had a voluminous correspondence with many people throughout Europe. People in what became the Church of England, Melanchthon of the Lutheran group, and people of Congregationalist persuasion in other cantons of Switzerland, were among his regular recipients of mail. The personal relationship of Calvin with these people, plus the touch of Geneva's law on the thousands who passed through its streets en route to their countries, put this law in a strategic position.

The laws on marriage and remarriage in Geneva were passed on November 13, 1561. They are to be found in the second volume of the untranslated *Calvini Opera*. Although they are not listed numerically, and although it is not necessary to quote the entire statute, the following general outline is given to help get the official position clearly before us.

The marriage ordinance opens with the heading, "What persons cannot marry without permission." [13] This section centered on the need for parental permission when people were under age. The portion that relates to our concern reads:

1. If it occurs that two young people have contracted marriage together on their own out of foolishness or lightheartedness, they should be punished and chastised, and such marriage should be rescinded at the behest of those who are in charge.[14]

The second section, then, dealt with " the persons who may marry without permission." [15] These were people who were over the age of twenty (for boys) or eighteen (for girls). Such individuals did not have to follow parental direction, but the law admonished: [16]

2. It will be more proper if they always let themselves be governed by the advice of their fathers.

This section further stated that:

3. All marriage promises be made honestly and in the faith of God: and not be dissolved by frivolous lightheartedness. . . . But at the request of one of the parties who claims to have been taken by surprise, the marriage should be rescinded.

The next eight sections of the ordinance are quite short. They are entitled, in order, " For what causes a promise may be rescinded," " That promises should be made simply," " The terms by which the marriage should be accomplished after the promise," " The marriage celebration," " The common dwelling of the husband with his wife," " The degree of blood relationship which prevents marriage," and " The degree of kinship." Under these headings, the following specific statements are of interest here:

4. That if there appears a promise between two capable persons, the marriage may not be rescinded but for two reasons: to wit, when there is sufficient proof that a girl who was supposed to be a virgin is not one; or if one of the parties should have a contagious and incurable disease.[17]

5. After the promise has been made, the marriage should not be deferred more than six weeks; otherwise, the parties should be called before the consistory the first day in order to be admonished. If they do not obey, they are then to be sent before the council in order to be forced to celebrate it.[18]

If the man or the woman decide that they do not want the marriage:

6. The minister should put the opposing one before the consistory the first day and admonish him to his part there.

In doing this, the feelings of the individuals involved were to be respected, for this was to be done in complete confidence " in order to avoid that somebody else make no rebuke or injury to some honest girl or the opposite." [19]

7. The announcements shall be published for three Sundays in the church before the marriage be concluded, having the signature of the first syndic, . . . in such a manner that the marriage can be made at the third publication. And if one of the parties should be of another parish, one must also have the good attestation of that place.[20]

8. The parties at the time they will be wed should come modestly to the church, without tambourines and minstrels, having an order and earnestness suitable to Christians; and [they should come] before the end of the bell-ringing so that the blessing of the marriage can be made before the sermon. If they are negligent, and if they come late, they should be sent back.

That it shall be permitted to celebrate marriages all the days: to wit, on working days at the service which appears suitable to the parties; on Sunday at the service at the beginning of the day . . . and that of 3:00 P.M.: except the days when the Lord's Supper is being celebrated, so that there be no distraction and that everybody be better disposed to receive the Sacrament.[21]

The last two sections of the ordinances concerned the grounds on which a marriage could be declared null, and the grounds on which a marriage could be "rescinded."

9. If it happens that a wife complains that he who has taken her in marriage is bewitched by nature, not being able to have company with a wife, and that this is found true by confession or visitation: that the marriage be declared void, and the wife declared free, and the man be warned not to abuse any more women.

Similarly, if the man complains that he cannot live with his wife for any defect in her body, and that she does not want to suffer in order that it be remedied: after having known the truth of the fact, the marriage should be declared void.[22]

10. If a husband accuses his wife of adultery, and he proves it to her by witnesses or sufficient indications and he requests to be separated by divorce, that they grant

it to him: and by this means he has the power to marry
or whatever seems to him best, although he could be
compelled to pardon his said wife: but this is not to be
insisted upon to restrain him beyond his good pleasure.

Although formerly the right of the wife was not equal
with that of the husband in cases of divorce, since according to the witness of the apostle the obligation is
mutual and reciprocal in reference to cohabitation of
the bed, and in this the wife is no more subject to the
husband than the husband to the wife, it follows that if
a man is convicted of adultery and the wife asks to be
separated from him, and they cannot be reconciled by
good admonitions, it shall be authorized.[23]

11. If a man by debauchment or by any bad affection
leaves and abandons the place of his residence, the wife
should make diligent inquiry in order to know where he
has withdrawn himself . . . (after she has done everything possible to bring him back), that the pursuit be
not abandoned until he has been denounced. He shall be
declared for three Sundays, fourteen days apart, so that
the term be six weeks. And the same shall be done three
times in the court of the lieutenant, and it shall be made
known to two or three of his closest friends or relatives,
if there are any. If he does not appear, the wife may go
to the nearest consistory thereafter, to request separation, and she shall be granted it, . . . and he who has
been rebellious shall be banned forever. (If this happens
a second time, the man is to be severely punished. The
third time, the wife is to have no further relation with
the man.) After diligent inquiry, when a year has passed
she can come to the consistory: and if it is known that
she needs to marry, after she has been exhorted, she may
be sent back to the council to have her swear an oath

that she does not know where he has gone, and the same shall be done with his closest relatives and friends. After that, the procedure shall be . . . to give liberty to the said wife to be able to remarry.[24]

The ordinance then goes on to say that if the wife leaves the husband and lives in a place of ill repute, he too is to do everything possible to bring her back. If all efforts fail and " she is found charged with the very strong suspicion of having been lecherous and having withdrawn to bad and suspect company, . . . the husband shall be granted his request for divorce." [25]

The ordinances closed with two interesting statements. One referred to the responsibility of man and wife to live together. The other referred to the responsibility of the consistory.

12. The married parties will not be permitted to live apart from each other. The wife, at the request of the husband, shall always be compelled to follow him, when he wants to change residence, or when he is forced to do so by necessity, under the condition that it is not a debauched man who leads her astray and into a strange land. (If he wished to live in a reasonable country, and as a good man, the wife must go too.)[26]

13. All matrimonial cases concerning the personal relationship, and not the goods, be treated in the first instance in the consistory: and that there, if an amiable settlement can be made, it be done in the name of God. If it is necessary to pronounce some juridical sentence, the parties shall be sent to the council with the declaration of the advice of the consistory, in order to have by it the definite sentence.[27]

Many things could be said about the comparison between these ordinances and modern American laws. The
fact of the engagement was taken far more seriously than
it is today. The relationship between the church court
(consistory) and the civil court (the council) was much
more intimate than that between today's session, vestry,
or trustees and the magistrate's court. Of special interest,
however, is the difference between this law and the laws
that will be seen in the next chapter.

It first must be observed that some writers have pictured
these laws — and by implication, Calvin — as much freer
than actually was true. In her book on Calvin, Georgia
Harkness states that Calvin allowed for divorce on several
grounds: adultery, impotence, desertion, and religious incompatibility.[28] William Cole also cites these grounds for
Calvin.[29] Cole obliquely refers to these laws as the source
of his information. In the ordinances as stated, it is clear
that adultery and desertion were grounds for divorce, but
there is no mention of religious incompatibility. Impotence was the basis for annulment, not for divorce. The
evidence Harkness gives for incompatibility is the case of
an Italian named Caracciolo. Caracciolo was married. He
was converted to Protestantism and fled to Geneva. His
Catholic wife refused to go with him.[30] Because of her refusal to change her religion and leave, Caracciolo was permitted to divorce and remarry.

If there is any other evidence that Calvin allowed for remarriage because of religious incompatibility, Harkness
does not mention it. I do not know of any. This instance
alone does not prove her point. Religious compatibility
was not the issue. This was a case of desertion interpreted
under the ordinance just listed as number twelve. The
fact that Caracciolo had moved to a "reasonable coun-

try " and that his wife did not accompany him would be sufficient to justify his divorce on the ground of desertion.

The desire of many to see Geneva in as modern a light as possible is understandable. However, it may have led some people to confuse strictness with legalism. No matter how broad one may wish Calvin to be, it cannot be denied that this law was quite strict. In the very first statement, there was the rule that nullified marriages contracted out of " foolishness or lightheartedness." Throughout the statements, there is the repetition of every type of rule to require husband and wife to do everything possible before a divorce. Here, there is no easy escape from an unhappy marriage.

The confusion between strictness and legalism lies in confusion about the approach to remarriage law. The crucial question concerns not the strictness of this law but the manner of its interpretation. For that, we must rely, in a moment, upon Calvin. Was his approach legalistic or dynamic? Was this law speaking to the real problem, or was it irrelevant and unrealistic?

That the law was not legalistic and was relevant is first seen in the use these ordinances make of " time." In modern laws, there is a one-year waiting period. It seems to have the prime virtue of helping the minister prevent hasty divorce and remarriage. The use of time in the Geneva ordinances had practically nothing to do with the minister. In fact, the mood seemed to be one of speed. It would be hard to imagine an American couple getting into trouble with church authorities because they did not get married soon enough! Yet, in Geneva, woe to the person who waited more than six weeks.

I suspect that this desire for speed had its base in Calvin's view of marriage. If marriage was seen as part of one's calling under God, then, when one was ready and declared it, he should not delay. Calvin did not put it in these words, but it is logical to say that when " readiness for marriage " was evident, that marriage should be consummated forthwith. Not to do so would be to leave God as well as the bride at the altar!

The waiting periods that the law imposed — in one instance ten years, and in another, one — had to do strictly with the culture of the day. In the twentieth century, thanks to telephone and telegraph, it is much easier to locate missing persons than in Calvin's generation. With the slow means of both transportation and communication, ten years was arrived at as a minimum figure to ensure that a desertion had indeed taken place. The rule was used, not to hinder remarriage, but to protect the person who might be wrongly divorced. By the same token, the one-year rule was stipulated as being sufficient for trying to reconcile a husband who had become a renegade.

The use of " time " in these ordinances does not prove that they had the Christian view. The fact is, however, that these ordinances are consistent with that view.

The recognition of the place of both the church and the couple is also a distinction between these laws and those of today. In fact, one weakness of the Geneva law may be that it does not sufficiently describe the minister's role in remarriage. In Geneva, it was the consistory and not the individual minister who was involved. Note how the regulations for announcing an intended wedding, for having the marriage within the context of the corporate worship of the church, for considering the parents, and for going to the consistory, all speak to the community aspect of divorce and remarriage.

On the other hand, the position of the individual was

not lost. A tremendous point is made in these rules of the equal individual rights of the woman with the man. Although some recognize this to a degree, there is a tendency to overlook it. For example, Georgia Harkness observes that the woman had to work harder than the man in case of desertion.[31] But this seeming difference can be fully explained by the culture of the day. In a time when it was only the man who was apt to be in business, in a day when only the man was apt to travel to different countries alone, it would hardly occur to anyone to state the same detailed regulations for finding a missing wife as for a missing husband. Women may have been regarded less highly than men in Geneva, but this law is not the proof. To the contrary, the several uses of the phrase " as in the case of the man " and the recognition of the differences between male and female situations are evidence of awareness for the reality of the individual.

That this law was not legalistic must be argued on the basis of Calvin's writings. In itself, though, the law inherently suggests that is was not. The very fact that desertion was a ground for divorce implied a nonlegalistic reading of the Gospel; Jesus spoke only of adultery. Further, one reason for allowing a woman to remarry after divorce was knowledge of her " need to marry." A rule based on such a dynamic, human need is not a legalistic rule.

Because they are hopelessly out of touch with the political and cultural framework in twentieth-century America, the Geneva ordinances would not be adequate as such for today. Nor is there any recognition here of the need for " realized forgiveness." Nevertheless, the strange part is that this law has more in common with the position that I have stated above than do the modern church laws. The use of time, the recognition of the corporate and individual factors, and the nonlegalistic approach make this true.

The important point is to recognize that Calvin saw marriage as a relationship that created a new organism — the one flesh. He saw divorce as the term that recognized the tearing or rupture in the organism of the husband-wife relationship. These ordinances are a legitimate statement, in the form of law, of Calvin's position. They also demonstrate that, for the Reformer, there can be a consistent and logical relation between one's theology and one's church discipline.

To understand how this law should be interpreted, Calvin's own understanding is important. It would be possible to go into his whole theology with reference to this one point, but that would take us far afield. It will be sufficient for us to ask some questions of Calvin's approach to the remarriage law:

1. What is Calvin's view of church law?
2. What is his understanding of the specific laws on remarriage?
3. What is his view of adultery?
4. What is his view of the place of culture?
5. Does he have a Christian understanding of time?
6. What is his view of community or corporateness?
7. Does the realization of forgiveness fit consistently with his position?

Church law. For Calvin, the purpose of church law, or discipline, was to maintain the integrity and the purity of the fellowship and to provide for the "edification" of people. His basic aim in church laws was to help acquire and maintain the relationship of people with God and with one another.

The specific guide as to what would help create and preserve this integrity centered in the Lord's Supper. The Lord's Supper was the actual experience in which the community aspect of life — in this case, Christian life — became manifest. In this regard he once wrote Farel:

> Consider how wretched would be the state and condition of the church if she could be compelled to receive to the partaking in so great a mystery those of whom she is altogether ignorant or perhaps regards with suspicion. And to say nothing of the church, how shall the minister discharge this onerous duty, unless he proceeds upon some fixed and certain methods for separating the worthy from the unworthy communicants.[32]

To put it in the language of today, Calvin was concerned that the church be the place where people could feel that they were not cut off from God. It was to be the place where they could feel his love. The purpose of discipline was to help make the church be that place.

Specific law. Specific law, for Calvin, was to be understood dynamically, not legalistically. He would have agreed with the lawyers quoted earlier. Wherever one looks, there is evidence to support this approach on the part of Calvin.

In his little book, *Instruction in Faith*, Calvin wrote, " Observance of the law, therefore, is not a work that our power can accomplish, but it is a work of a spiritual power."[33] He elsewhere spoke of " fulfilling " the law[34] and of listening to the law.[35]

These phrases suggest that the law of God is something more than a set of rules. There is in the rules something to be discovered called the " law." This law is not something just to be obeyed but to be " fulfilled." Fulfillment is a dynamic word. In addition, such fulfillment is to be experienced, not by works, but by spiritual power. Throughout, Calvin's references to law deny a legalistic approach.

Again, in the *Institutes,* he is very specific. " Paul . . . affirms that ' the law is spiritual.' " [36] He then goes on to say:

> It must be observed, in the second place, that the commands and prohibitions always imply more than the words express, but this must be so restricted, that we may not make it a Lesbian rule.[37]

Thus, Calvin did not allow for subjectivism. To prevent both legalism and subjectivism in the interpretation of law, he gave three rules. First, the exposition of the law must be directed to the design or intent of the precept. That is, what was the subject of the rule? Second, the exposition must consider the result of the rule. Third, the explanation must state the opposite meaning of the rule. Every " thou shalt not " implies a " thou shalt."

The view of adultery. Specifically with regard to adultery, Calvin spelled out this dynamic interpretation of the law.

In answer to the question. " What is adultery? " he said: " It is the crime of violating that fidelity which husbands and wives owe to each other and which they have reciprocally promised." [38] In the next question, he went on to say, " Every impure connection between persons who are not united by the tie of marriage, and every action, word, and thought which is inconsistent with decency and chastity " are part of adultery.[39]

Further, in the law, Calvin made it clear that the responsibility for granting a divorce did not rest upon one man. In his commentary he said:

> As he [Moses] declares that it is not in the power of
> the husband to dissolve the marriage, so likewise he for-
> bids all others to confirm by their authority unlawful di-
> vorces; for the magistrate abuses his power when he
> grants permission to the husband to divorce his wife.[40]

Again, in his commentary on the Gospels, we read:

> The bond of marriage is too sacred to be dissolved at
> the will or, rather, at the licentious pleasure, of man.
> Though the husband and the wife are united by mutual
> consent, yet God binds them by an indissoluble tie, so
> that they are not afterward at liberty to separate. An ex-
> ception is added, except on account of fornication: for
> the woman who has basely violated the marriage vow
> is justly cast off; because it was by her fault that the tie
> was broken and the husband set at liberty.[41]

This final statement seems to indicate that divorce is
wrong when carried out by one individual, but that there
are certain conditions — i.e., fornication — when the *presence of divorce* can be recognized to have taken place.
When these conditions prevail, the innocent party is free
to remarry. The opposite of forbidding adultery was the
blessing of the true marriage relationship.

The dynamic approach to adultery, as opposed to seeing
it as just a physical act, is confirmed by Calvin's commentary on the books of Moses, where he discusses the Tenth
Commandment:

> It has been said before that, agreeably to the nature
> of the lawgiver, the inward purity of the heart is every-
> where required, and, therefore, that under the head of
> adultery, not only are filthy acts prohibited, but secret
> unchastity also.[42]

This commandment held, said Calvin, that all that had
been previously commanded should be performed with

the sincere affection of the heart. Adultery, then, was seen by Calvin as a spiritual affair that had physical expression. For him, adultery was the way a marriage died; for, from the standpoint of the moral law, an adulterer was dead.

The question now arises as to how this permission to remarry divorced persons was reconciled with his strong objections to divorce. Divorce tears oneself apart, and this, for Calvin, was contrary to the way God made us. In discussing this issue about the Biblical view, we said that it is one thing to hate divorce, and another to ask what to do after divorce has been seen. Whether or not Calvin made this distinction, the records are not clear. That divorce did happen, even though it was contrary to nature, is definite. That he allowed for remarriage is equally definite.

With regard to the guilty party in divorce, Calvin's view seems ambiguous. He nowhere argues the question as to whether or not it is impossible to speak of an innocent party. From his theology, he could be expected to object to that term. Regardless, he seems to go along with the customary word usage. At the same time, it seems clear that there was some latitude in his view of "innocency." In the case of remarrying the person whose wife remained Catholic, who got the divorce? It was the husband who committed the act that resulted in the break. Calvin undoubtedly would consider the husband innocent on the grounds that, having seen the true light, the convert left Romanism. To say this, however, is to hold that the meaning of "innocent party" is subject to various interpretations even for Calvin.

There can be no question that Calvin had a strict view of the law. Equally, there can be no question that the dynamic aspect of that law was as much a part of his strict interpretation as the letter of the law.

Culture. Culture, and its relation to the faith, was recognized by Calvin and Luther in a way unique to their time. In a sense, it was the very lack of recognition of the place and influence of culture that made the Reformation necessary. As indicated in a previous quote from Calvin, he felt that culture always determined the mode by which the Word of God became known. In addition, he saw that culture influenced the way individuals would understand what the Word of God is.

This view of culture fits closely what we have been saying about the essential element in remarriage, " realized forgiveness." Culture is what people do. It is the way they act and think. It involves history. Therefore, it can be described and measured.

The truth of the presence of God is not just a matter of culture. For Calvin, it is a revelation that bursts in on one. In our context, it is the experience of fullness. A person cannot free himself from what happened in the past, Calvin would argue; but in the presence of God, he can be free from the chains the past might have on him.[43] In the area of remarriage, this would mean that people cannot alter the fact of divorce in the past. What people can do is realize the presence of God in their lives and be freed from bondage to that divorce.

Time. " Time " is not discussed at great length by Calvin in the fashion of modern theologians. Yet, one short phrase gives the needed hint about his view of time.

At one point in his *Institutes,* Calvin discussed faith and the fact that it is first by faith that one possesses Christ. By that same faith, he showed that the benefits of Christ are enjoyed. In the course of the discussion, he wrote this sentence: " Yet, when we speak of faith as the origin of repentance, *we dream not of any space of time* which it employs in producing it; but we intend to signify, that a man cannot truly devote himself to repentance, unless he knows himself to be of God." [44] (Italics mine.)

By this sentence, Calvin implied that how one thinks of time will determine how one thinks of the whole Christian faith. Note that he rejected any image of a space of time such as the straight line or the circle.

It is not necessary to attempt a long documentation of this point. Directly and by implication, there is abundant evidence that Calvin had a Christian view of time.[45]

Community or corporateness. The law in Geneva showed the result of Calvin's awareness of community. It was not the individual minister that made the important decision, it was the community through its elected representatives. It was to the community that a proposed marriage was announced in advance. It was to the community that a divorce request was presented for six weeks.

This view of community did not come by accident. It is at the heart of Calvin's thinking. Unfortunately, there is a popular view of Calvin as a rugged individualist. This view has missed his most important contribution. It has also warped a proper understanding of his position. His insight about corporateness is quite lacking today. Since this view is particularly important with regard to the remarriage of divorced persons and is greatly ignored, considerable attention must be given to it here.

There are many who challenge the idea that community or corporateness is fundamental to Calvin's theology. Individualistic capitalism has been credited to Calvin. The criticism of Calvinistic churches has been that they did not seem to be aware that there is a corporate dimension to life.

One could well observe, for example, that the word

"corporateness" is not used as such by Calvin. It could be replied that he never uses the word "individualism" either. Nevertheless, many modern studies of Calvin are based on a view of rugged individualism. In speaking about his interpretations of the Ten Commandments, for example, Dr. Harkness says:

> Yet, before the Ten Commandments can be obeyed, they must be interpreted. Calvin saw this; and he had no idea of admitting the right of everybody to interpret the Decalogue at will. As the rest of the Bible was written to show the true meaning of God's law as revealed to Moses, so must later expositions make clear the applications of these commandments. But how? Calvin had a simple answer. He believed firmly that God had imparted to his elect servant, John Calvin, the wisdom to do this for the Genevan Church and for all who sought his counsel. Through Calvin's lips, God spoke.[46]

The above quote suggests the way Dr. Harkness and others have approached Calvin. For her, the basis for understanding Calvin was his view of Christ. This results in seeing all sorts of inconsistencies in Calvin's statements. For Dr. Harkness, Calvin's view on remarriage is itself a surprising development in the light of his culture and thinking.

Actually, his views on remarriage are not surprising if one is ready to find another center from which to study Calvin. This other center is not Calvin's view of Christ, but his view of the Christian community — the church.

Calvin rejected the Roman Catholic *use* of the analogy between marriage and the relationship of Christ to the church as evidence for a sacramental view of marriage. However, he did not reject the analogy. On the contrary, he saw it as evidence of the social or corporate dimension of man's life. A husband and wife "by the bond of marriage have become one man." [47] For, said Calvin, "the strong affection which a husband ought to cherish toward his wife is exemplified by Christ, and an instance of that unity which belongs to marriage is declared to exist between himself and the church." [48]

Hence, the corporate nature of life was clear in marriage — a man and woman were bound up in each other as one. So, Christ and the church were bound up in each other as the "body of Christ." In his writings, Calvin appears to have moved both ways. From his awareness of corporateness in marriage, he moved to a view of corporateness in all of life. From his awareness of corporateness in all of life, he moved to a view of corporateness in marriage law.

Such authorities as McNeill, the historian, and Karl Barth, the theologian, support this view of the corporate dimension in Calvin. With them, the emphasis is not his Christology but his view of the church. The individual Christ is to be understood on the basis of the corporate view of life as given by Calvin throughout his writings.

Sadly, Calvinists have, by and large, reversed this correct order. Barth also began this way when he wrote *Christian Dogmatics*. His reversal to a *Church Dogmatics* is in line with the spirit of the Reformer.

Realized forgiveness. Calvin does not list "realized forgiveness" as one of the conditions for remarriage. That does not mean, however, that the experience of realized forgiveness was not a part of his situation just as it is of ours. Not just in connection with marriage, but in connection with life as a whole, Calvin discussed under the general heading of absolution the way forgiveness becomes real.

Calvin's thinking seemed to be that one made his way back to the fellowship and to God first by confession and then by being aware of absolution from his sin. If this awareness of God's forgiveness did not seem real through the public worship service, then the individual was to go to the pastor. Whether public or private, Calvin saw the minister as the channel of absolution. The power that came through preaching was, in his theology, just that: that the truth of the gospel of forgiveness became real to the hearer through the minister.

How did this forgiveness become real? It became real first by making restitution for the wrongs that had been done. If someone had sinned against another person, Calvin cited the admonition about leaving one's gift at the altar and first going to square accounts with that person.[49] If the sin was against the church as a whole, the church as a whole had to be asked for forgiveness. It was the church as a whole that showed the forgiveness by admitting the sinner again to the Lord's Supper.[50] If the sin was against God — and, fundamentally, this meant every sin — repentance before God was needed.

The second step in making forgiveness real was genuine " mortification." By " mortification " he meant " sorrow of the mind, and the terror experienced from a knowledge of sin and a sense of the divine judgments." [51] In other words, if forgiveness is ever to be real, a person has to be genuinely aware of needing it and of being sorry for what happened. Calvin had rather picturesque images of what this meant, but they can be attributed to the culture of the time. The important point is that no one can have a real awareness of forgiveness if there is not first real awareness of guilt.

The third step in making forgiveness real was " vivication." " Vivication " meant seeing the reality of God's love as clearly as the reality of one's own sin. Practically, this meant that a man should " desire and endeavor to live a holy and pious life, as though it were said, that a man dies to himself, that he may begin to live to God." [52]

Although Calvin never used the term " realized forgiveness," he described something like it. He did not speak of this directly with regard to marriage. For him, marriage was but one of the many areas in which a person could sin. Since the problem of remarriage was not as prominent in his day as the fear of eternal damnation, it is understandable that he centered his comments on the latter. However, the fact that his views fit logically with the approach of this book should give reason for questioning the modern church laws.

In a sense, it is both harder and easier to get Luther's approach to remarriage than Calvin's. It is harder, because there is no great body of church law to place behind Luther and compare with the present in the sense of the Geneva law. Further, Luther was the publicist of the Reformation; Calvin the systematician. Luther wrote magnificent tracts and books for the public. There was a beauty and an almost mystical insight to his works — including his translation of the Bible — that is lacking in Calvin. Calvin had a style, but it was the style of the legal mind placing his arguments in sequence.

As with Calvin, Luther was against divorce. Yet, late in his life, Luther seemed almost scandalous in his liberal views on the marriages of some of the German princes. The Bible said nothing against polygamy; hence, neither did Luther.

Luther had three views with regard to remarriage. Underlying them all was the belief that the fall of man had corrupted marriage just as it had corrupted every dimension of life. Therefore, Luther, with Calvin and the Bible, was against sin and against divorce. Yet, when it happened, what did one do about it?

Luther found it difficult to accept divorce for one who already was a Christian, but he did accept it for adultery and desertion. That was his first view. His second view was that, when a person was married to an unbeliever, there was the Pauline privilege about being "unevenly yoked." In the third place, Luther did not stress the matter of remarriage by only the innocent party. The Gospel was silent on that point; hence, by what authority should the church invoke it?

For our purposes here, the great value of Luther's position was not that he did remarry divorced people but that he clearly saw the corporate aspect of all of life. There was no place in his thought for unbridled individualism. Marriages were basically arranged because marriages were an affair of the total family. Further, with regard to divorce, he saw it as a matter for the whole of society. In writing on the Sermon on the Mount,[53] he said:

> What is the proper procedure for us nowadays in matters of divorce? I have said that this should be left to lawyers and made subject to the secular government. For marriage is a rather secular and outward thing, having to do with wife and children, house and home, and with other matters that belong to the realm of the government.

This quote relates in part to the question of legal jurisdiction of divorce cases. Luther felt it lay in the state. The question of jurisdiction is not important here. Vital is the recognition that in Luther as well as Calvin, there was a deep awareness of the corporate dimension in all of living.

In the Church of England, the influence of the Roman Catholic position was evident during the Reformation period. Under that point of view, divorce was seen only as a condescension to the flesh. Rome did not allow divorce. Henry VIII wanted one. Hence, the shift came. Until as late as 1938, the law in England allowed divorce on the grounds of adultery only.

Again, within the Church of England, it is important to note the awareness of the community understanding of life. Marriage was within the church. An individual could not get married by himself. Through the bishop, the church, and not just the lone priest, was much in evidence in the matter of marriage. The priest had to refer any questions put to him. The rebellion of Henry VIII is evidence of this very point. The king could not marry out of the church. Hence, as it were, he changed churches. Had the concept of the community and cultural impact of the church not been strong, he would have acted as any individualistic American. He would have gone to a justice of the peace to get married and gone back to church the next Sunday with no sense of inconsistency. This would have been easier on his wives too.

Before turning to the actual laws of some present-day churches, a few observations can be made by way of summary.

First, the "dynamic" approach of church law is the only one that is relevant to the problem of remarriage and that is supported by church history. It is the only one relevant to the problem because the legalistic approach completely misses the real issue involved. It is the only one supported by church history and the Bible. The prophets of the Bible and history have constantly had to fight the legalistic approach. We saw it in the Old Testament and in Jesus. We saw it in Calvin.

Secondly, realized forgiveness is the factor that establishes the possibility of remarriage. This point was discovered in the actual experiences of pastoral care. It was not only consistent with, but it had support in, Calvin. It is not only consistent with, but it has its Christian base in, the Bible.

Thirdly, corporateness, or an awareness of community, must be recovered if marriage is to have any meaning and if the answer of the church to divorce is to be relevant. This truth is the contribution of the Reformation period to our day. It was clear in Calvin, in Luther, and in the Church of England. The truth is confirmed by the experience of actual pastoral work. Lack of awareness of the community has resulted in lack of relevance on the part of ministers and church officers in dealing with the couple who come to the Christian community. With these thoughts in mind, let us now look at the modern laws themselves.

6

THE DENOMINATIONAL LAWS

At present there are three general approaches to the question of the remarriage of divorced persons. These approaches are dictated by the three general types of church polity — Episcopalian, Presbyterian, and Congregational.

The Episcopal system features several levels of authority. An individual clergyman holds the power at each level. The most obvious example is the Roman Catholic Church with its hierarchy of priest, bishop, pope. The Methodist Church also has this system. The other extreme is the Congregationalist system, in which full authority is vested in each local congregation. At the present time, some " primitive Baptist " churches are the purest examples of this form. Between these two groups is the Presbyterian system, which has representative government. As in the Episcopacy, there is a hierarchy or gradation of authority; but it is a hierarchy of councils as opposed to individuals. The choosing of members of this hierarchy remains within the power of the congregation and the presbytery — the two basic units of the Presbyterian system.

The approach of the Episcopal system to the matter of remarriage tends to be one of the individual in power directing the priests as to what they may do. As a result, a parish priest has a highly structured framework within which to operate. Canon Warner, of the Church of England, quoted a comment by the then Bishop of York concerning a bill in parliament as follows:

> The Bill, expressly in Clause 11, gives liberty to the clergyman, which liberty, of course, he may exercise in accordance with directions drawn up for him by the Church itself. . . . The Archbishops clearly reserved the right of the Church to give orders to the clergy. These " orders " were, in fact, given by the Bishops acting on the resolution agreed upon by all four Houses of Convocation in 1936.[54]

That individual British clergymen did violate the rules of the bishops is clear [55] and that there is considerable discussion about the remarriage law in England is evident to all who follow the television and news releases of the controversy. Nevertheless, the Archbishop's statement clearly indicated the tendency of this approach to give the minister a maximum of security and limited freedom in dealing with a couple who request marriage after divorce.

The Congregationalist system leans in the direction of no structure at all with regard to marriage. The *Manual of the Congregational Christian Churches* is explicit in stating two principles of church polity: " One is the entire completeness of each local church for its own government; and the other is the principle which relates to all those duties and privileges which grow out of the relation of one church to another." [56] The *Manual* asserts that, in the course of the history of Congregationalism, the focuses of freedom and fellowship have never been challenged but have had differing degrees of emphasis. Chapter XXXIII says in part: " The earlier associations of ministers, in the

Congregational fellowship, differed from those of today in being chiefly voluntary clubs of ministers that correspond somewhat to our present-day ministers meetings, clubs, or brotherhoods. The association of churches and ministers, however, has come to be more than a voluntary organization." [57]

In so far as the pure Congregational system is followed, the individual minister has a great deal of freedom. The lack of structure, however, results in great differences in practice in different churches. It also gives increasing opportunity for pure subjectivism as the only basis for dealing with remarriage.

The Presbyterian system has elements both of structure and of individual freedom. It has the problem both of giving too much structure and of experiencing too much subjective judgment. In the history of the church, the emphasis at times was on the element of structure. At other times, the emphasis was on personal freedom.

With this general picture of the types of church government, consider now the specific laws.

The Present Law of the Episcopal Church

The present Episcopal law in America can be found in Canon 17 and Canon 18 of the *Constitution and Canons for the Government of the Protestant Episcopal Church in the United States of America*. The following excerpts were taken from the printing of that law for the General Convention held in 1958.

Canon 17. Of the Solemnization of Holy Matrimony [58]
Section 1. Every Minister of this Church shall conform to the laws of the State governing the creation of the civil status of marriage, and also to the laws of this Church governing the solemnization of Holy Matrimony.

Section 2. Conditions of Marriage

C. He shall have ascertained that at least one of the parties has received Holy Baptism.

D. He shall have instructed the parties as to the nature of Holy Matrimony.

E. Three days' notice before a marriage, if waived, means that a minister must report his action in writing to the Ecclesiastical Authority immediately.

Section 3. A declaration of intent has to be signed to show that the position of *The Book of Common Prayer* is understood.

Section 4. Any minister may decline to solemnize a marriage.

Section 5. No minister of the Church shall solemnize the marriage except in accordance with these Canons.

Section 6. No minister of the Church shall solemnize the marriage of any person who has been the husband or wife of any other person then living whose marriage has been annulled or dissolved by the civil court, except as hereinafter in these Canons provided; nor shall any member of this Church enter upon a marriage when either of the contracting parties has been the husband or the wife of any other person then living whose marriage has been annulled or dissolved by a civil court as hereinafter in these Canons provided.

Canon 18. Of the Regulations Respecting Holy Matrimony

Section 2(a). Any person, being a member of this Church in good standing, whose marriage has been annulled or dissolved by a civil court of competent jurisdiction may apply to the Bishop or Ecclesiastical Authority of the Diocese or Missionary District in which such person is canonically resident for a judgment as to his or her marital status in the eyes of the Church. And any person, being a member of this Church in good standing, who desires to marry a nonmember of the Church whose previous marriage has been dissolved or annulled by a civil court of competent jurisdiction may apply to the Bishop or Ecclesiastical Authority of the Diocese or Missionary

District in which he or she is canonically resident, for permission to be married by a Minister of this Church, provided in both cases that the judgment of the civil court has become final and that at least one year shall have elapsed from the date that the decree became final. Such application should be made at least thirty days before a contemplated marriage.

Section 2(b). If the Bishop or Ecclesiastical Authority is satisfied that the parties intend a true Christian marriage, he may refer the application to his Council of Advisors, or to the Court if such has been established by diocesan action. The Bishop or Ecclesiastical Authority shall take care that his or its judgment is based upon and conforms to the doctrine of this Church, that marriage is a physical, spiritual, and mystical union of a man and woman created by their mutual consent of heart, mind, and will hereto, and is a Holy Estate instituted of God and is in intention lifelong; but when any of the facts set forth in Canon 17, Section 2, Clause b (laws about consanguinity) are shown to exist or to have existed which manifestly establish that no marriage bond as is recognized by this Church exists, the same may be declared by proper authority. No such judgment shall be construed as reflecting in any way upon the legitimacy of children or the civil validity of the former relationship.

The Development of the Episcopal Law

Over the years, the law in the Episcopal Church has been subject to considerable debate. There have been three general points of view. One group has held that there should be no remarriage at all. This position could be argued, within the Episcopal framework, from two points of view. Persons who held to a literalistic interpretation of the Scripture and who did not allow the escape clause in Matthew would be against remarriage. This group would have much in common with persons of similar legalistic persuasion in every other denomination.

Those who held to the sacramental view of marriage would oppose remarriage on the basis that such marriage was an impossibility. The advocates of this position would find much in common with the Roman Catholic Church.

A second group has admitted remarriage on the basis of adultery. This has been the traditional and generally accepted position in the history of most churches. Particularly in the Church of England, this basis for divorce and remarriage is generally under attack. Some argue that there should be no basis for remarriage; others argue that there should be a broad base. But both, from their different motives, attack the use of " adultery " as the ground for remarriage.

A third group has argued that any ground for remarriage is legitimate as long as the remarriage was approved, officially, by the bishop or his appointed representative. This position grows out of a premise that it is the church that fundamentally interprets both the Bible and the human situation. It is the church that has the " power of the keys " vested in the bishop. Hence, through the approval of the church, the condition is created for a remarriage.

Since the establishing of the Episcopal Church in the colonies, there have been changes in the law on remarriage that reflect this debate. The over-all meaning of these changes will be seen when these laws are compared with those of other denominations. In and of themselves, the shifts are also interesting.

Initially, the church law on remarriage was taken directly from the Church of England. After the Revolution and in the course of the early years of America, the Episcopal Church had all it could do to become established as an independent church. It not only had to sever its ties with England, it also had to adjust to the lack of state support. Further, it had to overcome the popular suspicion of its doings that grew from its initial connection with the established powers in England. Hence, in 1808, the decision was made to abide by the rules that had come from England. Remarriage was allowed, but only in the case of adultery and for the innocent party. The resolution read: " Resolved that it is the sense of this Church that . . . the Ministers of this Church shall not unite in matrimony any person who is divorced unless it be on account of the other party having been guilty of adultery." [59] This resolution, in 1808, was the only pronouncement of the General Convention on the subject of remarriage until 1868.

In 1868, the Convention passed another resolution that prohibited the remarriage of divorced people, except on the ground of adultery and on proof of innocency. But it made a few clarifying remarks. This law was to apply only to divorces where both parties were still living. If one had been divorced, and the wife or husband died, the survivor could then remarry. Also, the law did not apply if " two parties, once divorced, [were] seeking to be united again."

In the period around 1868, there must have been considerable difference in practice when it came to remarrying. There was a resolution at the Convention of 1877 which was in answer to a question of discipline. Should or should not the ministers who were remarrying people on other grounds than those stated be called to account? It was held that the " joint resolutions heretofore passed by the General Convention have never been deemed to have, and ought not to be construed as having, the force of law, but as being merely the expression of an opinion." [60] The Convention then repealed the Canon of 1868 and enacted, in part, the following principles: [61]

1. A marriage is not lawful if not done according to God's Word.

2. A marriage after divorce is not lawful except in the case of an innocent party where the cause was adultery, unless two divorced persons are wishing to reunite.

3. If any Minister of this Church shall have reasonable cause to doubt whether a person desiring of being admitted to Holy Baptism, or to Confirmation, or to the Holy Communion, has been married otherwise than as the Word of God and discipline of this Church allow, such Minister, before receiving such person to these ordinances, shall refer the case to the Bishop for his godly judgment thereupon; provided, however, that no Minister shall in any case, refuse the Sacraments to a penitent person in imminent danger of death.

4. Questions concerning the remarriage of divorced persons were to be referred to the Bishop.

These regulations could be considered the first actual laws of the Episcopal Church in America on the matter of remarriage. Among other things, they reflect that, even within as structured a government as the Episcopal system, interpretation is necessary. It was not enough to have simply the law. There had to be an approach to the law. These statements in 1877 had the force of providing the way in which the interpretation was to be sought. They also had the force of protecting the church as a whole against people who would violate the laws concerning marriage but still enjoy all the other benefits of the church (e.g., Communion).

From 1877 until 1904, there were no further changes in the church canon. In 1883, however, there was an attempt to get the restrictions reviewed. The pressure for a stringent ruling was great, and report after report was lost by only the slightest margin. Upon suggestion of the House of Bishops, a compromise proposal was finally adopted that added a time requirement of one year after the divorce, review of each case by an ecclesiastical authority, and permission from that authority.[62]

In 1916, a commission suggested greater instruction in the area of marriage for both clergy and laity. On the ground that the Biblical exceptions for divorce were questionable, the commission then recommended no remarriage on any basis. The debate carried through until 1919, when the suggestion was defeated. Although there were other discussions and suggestions, the most significant study since the initial one of 1868 came in 1931. The Joint Commission on Remarriage and Divorce presented a majority report and a minority report.

The majority report suggested that anyone, after one year from the divorce, could apply to the ecclesiastical court. The resolution read:

> The court shall thereupon inquire into the characters and personalities of the parties to the previous and proposed marriages and the conduct of the parties concerned in the divorce, and whether or not the applicant did what he or she reasonably could have done to avoid the separation; and if after this inquiry, the court shall determine that the spiritual welfare of the applicant will be best served thereby, it may permit the marriage.[63]

The minority report was far more liberal. It argued that anyone should be allowed to apply, regardless of the date of the divorce. This report held that the court needed to see no more than that the character of the parties was good and to " determine whether the welfare of the parties and the good of society will be served by such recognition." [64] The final result was again a canon that allowed for remarriage on the ground of adultery if the party was innocent.

In 1943, an interesting proposal would have put the matter into the hands of a bishop to be decided in consultation with the couple's pastor, the couple themselves, a lawyer, a psychiatrist, or a physician. With these people, the bishop was to investigate the case with a view to seeing whether or not a previous *Christian* marriage had indeed been established. This too was defeated.

In 1946, the exception for adultery was repudiated, and only nullity was allowed as a base for remarriage. The bishop was empowered to have a court investigate each case, but the bishop made the ultimate decision. The ruling also added that the Division of Education and the Division of Christian Social Relations should work with ministers to have better education in this area. Finally, in 1958, the law as presented at the outset of this section was approved.

This canon, as seen in the light of the denomination's history, could be construed as representing a liberalizing trend. It does not restrict the bishop to the matter of adultery. Further, on the surface, the law seems to be quite aware of the community — the church. Nowhere is the minister left on his own. He refers to the bishop. In the last formulation, the bishop is not left to his own devices either. He must stand responsible for the ultimate decision, but he may turn to a properly appointed court. In his speaking, he is speaking for the church, and not as an individual who has amassed power.

Whether or not this sense of corporateness is more than on the surface, however, there is some doubt. The canon requires the bishop to pass his thoughts on to the court only if he approves. If he disapproves, the power is solely in his hands. Further, the thrust of this law is negative. It has eliminated the " innocent party " phrase (for who really is the innocent party?). But in so doing, it has established no positive guide as to what makes for readiness to marry.

In regard to the position of this book, the Episcopal law has much to recommend it. Yet its emphasis on the one-year law, its lack of opportunity for appeal on the part of the couple, and its silence on what makes for readiness to marry make it a law that is not yet adequate to the real issues in remarriage.

The Present Law of The Methodist Church

Because of its somewhat episcopal structure, to go into the history of The Methodist Church as fully as into that of the Episcopal Church would in some sense be duplication. The bishop is again the authority, although in the area of remarriage there appears to be greater responsibility taken by the local pastor than in the Episcopal Church. In addition, The Methodist Church has, with its system of bishops, a system of judiciaries. By appeal of a Conference, the judiciary can set aside a decision of a bishop when the issue is a question of law.

The law of the church is found in the *Discipline of The Methodist Church*. It reads as follows:

> No minister shall solemnize the marriage of a divorced person whose wife or husband is living and unmarried; but this rule shall not apply (1) to the innocent person when it is clearly established by competent testimony that the true cause for divorce was adultery or other vicious conditions which through mental or physical cruelty or physical peril invalidated the marriage vow, nor (2) to the divorced person seeking to be reunited in marriage. The violation of this rule concerning divorce shall be considered an act of maladministration.[65]

Of the four church laws presented here, this is the only one that still requires the innocence of the person concerned in remarriage. Although it does go beyond the strict Biblical exception to the divorce rule, this law still is unique in not having made the substantial change that is seen in the other denominations.

But it does have the value of indicating some of the factors that are involved in readiness for marriage. One is absence of guilt. A second is absence of guilt in the presence of certain situations that invalidated the marriage.

In view of what has been said about realized forgiveness, I would question seriously that there can ever be this " innocent person." [66] Yet, in being the only law that has not made the substantial change found in the other denominations, the Methodist position thus stands as the only one that fully recognizes the importance of guilt in the remarriage issue. That proper dealing with guilt is a prime necessity in all remarriage is established by the experiences in pastoral care.

Unfortunately, this law does not seem in any way to recognize the corporate nature of remarriage. In an otherwise generally excellent appendix on the family, the position of the church in divorce is reduced to one of a traffic cop. The church is to " depict the unhappy circumstances that are to await the divorced person." Nowhere does one find a place for the interaction between the church and the couple in meeting these problems. The awareness of the church as a living community involved in this relationship which is sensed in the Episcopal laws is quite lacking.

The Position of the United Lutheran Church in America

The present procedure of the United Lutheran Church in America was adopted at its convention in October, 1956. It is found in the minutes of that session and also in a subsequent publication, *Christian Guidance on Marriage and Family Life.* The regulations are entitled "Summary Statements on Marriage and Family Life." They were accepted as regulations to supersede those of 1930.

The "Statements" begin with a declaration that marriage is part of the order of creation. They go on to discuss the legitimacy and place of sexual relations, the responsibility to children, the wedding, the position of pastors, the responsibility for training in the home, and the view of the church on state marriage laws. Section 6, which discusses divorce and remarriage, is as follows:

> Where marriage failure and divorce occur among Christian people, the church should recognize its involvement in the failure and seek to lead all concerned to repentance and forgiveness. If it proves impossible or unwise in the light of Christian love and concern for the welfare of all involved to reconstitute the marriage, then the church should continue, in so far as possible, to minister to each person involved.
>
> If the question of the remarriage of a divorced person arises, pastors and congregations of the United Lutheran Church in America should make their decisions on the particular circumstances in each case, being guided by the following considerations: [67]
>
> a. While it is the Christian teaching that marriage is a lifelong, indissoluble union and that divorce and remarriage do violate God's order, nevertheless, God in his love does accept the sinner and deal with him according to his need. The church has recognized that marriage may be a remedy for sin and has seen in such Bible passages as Matt. 5:32; 19:9; and I Cor. 7:15 the possibility of re-

marriage, but it also knows that the final basis of decision is loving concern for man in his actual situation.

b. The divorced person seeking remarriage must recognize his responsibility in the breakup of the former marriage. He must give evidence of repentance and have made an effort to overcome his limitations and failures. He must have forgiven his partner in the former marriage, and he and his intended spouse must give assurance that he will fulfill his obligations to those involved in his former marriage.

c. The divorced person must give evidence of his Christian faith by his witness in the church and must have received adequate counsel and training in preparation for marriage. He must be prepared to undertake the full responsibilities of marriage in dependence upon God.

The Development of the Lutheran Position

The above rule was passed at the twentieth biennial Convention. The 1930 statement represents the other major statement in this area made by the denomination. This is in contrast to the Episcopalian and Presbyterian groups that have had numerous changes and discussions in the course of their history. (The term "law" is not quite accurate in the Lutheran Church. The rules on remarriage were passed at the Convention but are not unalterably binding on the local congregation. The nature of the Conventions is such, however, that we can legitimately compare these rules with the laws of the other denominatons.)

In an excellent report presented to the Convention in 1930, a review was made of the two justifications for remarriage after divorce — adultery and desertion. The report observed that adultery was generally accepted but that desertion had come under question. The report examined the texts from Paul (I Cor. 7:15) on which the desertion clause was based. Notice was also taken of the

fact that Paul was aware of Christ's teaching on the matter of divorce and seemed, here, to be trying to make a
practical application.

Despite the fact that the law of the church had been
abused, the report concluded that there was no reason
to change it. Instead, it held, " the Church can and should
protect itself by requiring a stricter adherence on the part
of both clergy and laity to the principles which govern its
attitude toward the remarriage of those who have been
divorced for desertion." [68] How this would be done remained to be seen. Hence it concluded, " What the United
Lutheran Church is now asked to do is to endorse as a
Church substantially what the former General Synod declared to be its position at its meeting in 1907 and use
what the former General Council declared to be its position at its meeting in 1903, and what is declared to be the
teaching of the Scriptures in the ' Lutheran Commentary.'" The statement then may be summarized as follows:

1. Marriage is a holy estate to be honored by all.

2. Pastors are to instruct people regularly about the
family and to seek to maintain a Christian conscience
about divorce.

3. While it is indispensable that a pastor in performing
a marriage comply with every civil requirement, we maintain that he is also accountable to God, and that he therefore not only has the right, but should feel constrained,
to refuse to perform any marriage which, so far as he had
had the opportunity after earnest endeavor to ascertain
the facts, is not in accordance with the divine requirements. The rite of Christian marriage is a service of the
Church and its distinctively religious character when performed by a minister of the Church should never be
subordinated to other considerations.

4. With respect to divorce we hold that marriage ac-

cording to the will of God is indissoluble and is normally terminated only by the death of either party. When it is otherwise dissolved the will of God is frustrated. In general, therefore, all divorce is to be condemned, and, wherever possible, avoided.

5. A great body of the leading thinkers of the Lutheran Church in the past have taught that the marriage bond is effectually dissolved by the sins of adultery and malicious desertion, and that, when a divorce has been legally granted for either of these causes, the innocent party is free to marry again. This position we now affirm.

6. With respect to the remarriage of divorced persons, the United Lutheran Church recommends to its constituent synods that they insist that their pastors abide by the rule that only the innocent party to a divorce which has been granted on scriptural grounds can be remarried under the auspices of the Lutheran Church during the lifetime of the other party, and then not until the expiration of a year after the divorce shall have been granted.

7. The matter of retaining within, or admitting to, the membership of the Church persons who have been divorced on other than scriptural grounds and who have remarried during the lifetime of the former husband or wife falls under the rule of discipline provided for by the constitution of the congregation. In all such instances pastors and church councils are exhorted to proceed with care and true spiritual wisdom, having proper regard for the Church's purity and honor, but also mindful of her mission to minister the means of grace so that sinners may be converted, restored, and saved.[69]

Of the four modern laws presented here, the present Lutheran statement has gone the farthest in speaking to the real issues in remarriage. Both the statement of 1930 and that of 1956 were preceded by a thorough and clear study of the problem. Account was taken of the church in the past, the problem of the present, and the responsibilities involved.

The 1930 statement appears to be stricter than that of 1956. It recognizes that the "innocent party" question cannot be decided on the basis of the divorce papers. Yet it still holds that only the innocent party can be remarried. How, within the framework of Lutheran theology, there can be an innocent party, the resolution does not say. Nor does the 1930 resolution appear to have the Christian concept of time. The passing of one year before remarriage is considered necessary. Further, within the context of the discussion, it is clear that the 1930 regulations saw no other basis for remarriage than divorce that followed adultery and desertion. Said the report: "Crime, sickness, cruelty, incompatibility of temper may make temporary separation expedient or necessary, but none of these causes in itself destroys the possibility of reconciliation." [70]

The current rule of the Lutheran Church on divorce comes very close to the position argued in this study. The statement of the law followed several years of study on marriage and family life. It was presented in the context of an excellent report that reviewed the theological, pastoral, Biblical, and personal dimensions of marriage, divorce, and remarriage. Because this report looked at what was actually happening in the remarriage issue, it is not surprising that it produced some very relevant answers.

The law does not sharply state realized forgiveness as necessary in the remarriage of divorced people. It comes very close to it, however, when it says that God "in his love does accept the sinner and deal with him according to his need." The resolution further states that the divorcee must have forgiven his partner in the previous marriage. This ability to forgive suggests a profound insight: viz., that the power to forgive others and the power to feel forgiven are related. Evidence that a person is free from bondage to his guilt is freedom to forgive others. This psychological truth is documented again and again in volumes on psychotherapy. Hence, this statement in the law is a guide that speaks to the real issue at hand.

Yet the weakness remains. This part of the law has missed the point of the divorcee's forgiveness. It states that God does love. It states that the divorcee must be aware and sorry for his own failure. It says nothing about feeling the presence of God's love in relation to the divorcee's failure.

With regard to corporateness or community, the present ruling is an advance over the 1930 version. The statement recognizes that there is more than just one party to the situation. It clearly recognizes that the church is as much involved as the couple or the minister. "Where marriage failure and divorce occur among Christian people, the church should recognize its involvement in the failure." Although the Episcopal Church canon showed keenness with regard to the reality of the church, even it did not express awareness of the sense of involvement that is shown in the present Lutheran position.

Where this rule is weak in the matter of corporateness, the Episcopal canon is strong. The Lutheran position does not take into full account the place of the minister in regard to remarriage. For all practical purposes, the minister is entirely on his own. The couple has no appeal from the minister's decision. The minister is the sole interpreter of the law at this point.

The Law in The United Presbyterian Church U.S.A.

To find the law in the Presbyterian Church, one must look in two sections of that denomination's Constitution.

The Confession of Faith (the first section) gives the general view of the denomination on marriage as a whole. The specific views are found in a lengthy (second) section called the " Directory for Worship."

The totally revised section of the Confession of Faith, which was adopted in 1953, reads as follows: [71]

1. Christian marriage is an institution ordained of God, blessed by our Lord Jesus Christ, established and sanctified for the happiness and welfare of mankind, into which spiritual and physical union one man and one woman enter, cherishing a mutual esteem and love, bearing with each other's infirmities and weaknesses, comforting each other in trouble, providing in honesty and industry for each other and for their household, praying for each other, and living together the length of their days as heirs of the grace of life.

2. Because the corruption of man is apt unduly to put asunder those whom God hath joined together in marriage, and because the Church is concerned with the establishment of marriage in the Lord as Scripture sets it forth, and with the present penitence as well as with the past innocence or guilt of those whose marriage has been broken; therefore as a breach of that holy relation may occasion divorce, so remarriage after a divorce granted on grounds explicitly stated in Scripture or implicit in the gospel of Christ may be sanctioned in keeping with his redemptive gospel, when sufficient penitence for sin and failure is evident, and a firm purpose of and endeavor after Christian marriage is manifest.

The rules for the approach to the remarriage of divorced persons are contained in Chapter XIV of the Directory for the Worship of God. General views of marriage are stated that apply to all situations. These points hold that marriage is ordained of God, that marriage is not a sacrament, that people of discretionary age and well certified to the minister may marry, that parental pressure is unwise, that spiritual and ecclesiastical compatibility is important, that the rights of possible children should be protected, that there is a corporate nature to marriage, that a certain liturgy is suggesed, that a register be kept, and that, when in doubt, a minister should consult a committee in presbytery (the official body to which a minister is responsible).

Because of the bearing on divorced persons, certain of these laws are as follows: [72]

> Section 5. Ministers are admonished to emphasize the need of spiritual and ecclesiastical compatibility in marriage. Lack of harmony on the part of the parents in the training of their children when they differ in the essentials of the faith endangers the happiness of a truly Christian home.
>
> Section 7. Marriage is of a public nature. The welfare of civil society, the happiness of families, and the credit of religion are deeply involved in it. Therefore, the purpose to marry ought to be sufficiently published a proper time previous to the solemnization of it, and it is recommended that the intention of the contracting parties shall be made known to the minister at least three days before the service of solemnization. All ministers are enjoined to exercise due care that in this matter neither the laws of God nor the community shall be transgressed. In order that the peace and comfort of families be not endangered and that no just objection lie against the marriage, the parties applying should be properly certified to the minister.

The rules that apply specifically to instances of divorce state that the minister should ascertain whether or not there is penitence for the past failure and a firm intention to make the new marriage succeed. Unless the presbytery approves a change, the minister must wait one year before performing a remarriage, and he must not remarry those who come from a communion that would not permit the remarriage. Where injustice might result, this last point may be waived. However, in all cases of doubt, the minister may apply to the presbytery. The actual wording of the law on remarrying divorced people reads: [73]

Section 10. Inasmuch as the Church must uphold the Christian home and the permanence of the marriage tie, and at the same time minister sympathetically to any who have failed in this holy relation, ministers who are requested to remarry divorced persons shall ascertain whether there is penitence for past sin and failure, and intention to enter, with the help of God, and through his Church, into a marriage of love, honor, forbearance, and loyalty, which will continue as long as both shall live.

To implement the opposition of the Church to hasty remarriage, a minister shall officiate at the remarriage of a divorced person only after a period of at least one year has elapsed from the date of granting of the divorce, except with the approval of presbytery or its authorized representative.

In the interests of Christian comity, ministers are advised not to unite in marriage a member of any other Christian communion whose marriage is known to the minister to be prohibited by the laws of the Church in which such person holds membership, unless the minister believes that his refusal would do injustice.

Section 11. Since marriage confers the blessing of the Church, its solemnization lays upon ministers of the Church a weighty responsibility. In cases where the interpretation of the laws of the Church is in doubt, ministers are entitled to the aid and counsel of their brethren in session and presbytery. To provide such aid and counsel, each presbytery may elect a committee on Christian marriage.

When a minister seeks the counsel of presbytery as to

a proposed marriage or remarriage, he shall submit all the papers and facts in the case, including his considered judgment, to presbytery or its authorized representative, which shall be judge of satisfactory evidence as to whether there are grounds for marriage or remarriage in keeping with the spirit and teachings of our Lord, Jesus Christ. The decision of presbytery shall be a matter of record.

Although this eleventh section pertains to all marriages, I have placed it with the regulations on remarriage. The greatest use of this law is in connection with cases of divorce or annulment.

The Development of the Presbyterian Law

In America, this law can be traced in a way that is not possible in the other groups mentioned. Because of its dependence on England, the Episcopal view did not gain focus until 1868. The United Lutheran Church was formed in this century. By contrast, the Presbyterian Church, as an entity in America, began before the American Revolution. The present Presbyterian law on remarriage has a direct connection to the laws prior to the Revolution. For this reason, the study of this development gives a sweep that is somewhat unique.

It is obvious from the above law that the minister has great freedom and great power. He can remarry anyone where one year has elapsed, when there is penitence, and when there is good intention with regard to the future. Who is the sole judge of these attitudes? The minister. Unless the minister appeals for help, no one can cross him except in the matter of the one-year waiting period.

By contrast, the official position of the early church in America was both definite and rigid. Dr. Leonard Trinterud has made an excellent study of early Presbyterianism. He observes that marriage was allowed only on Biblical (particularly Old Testament) grounds. Throughout the colonial period, litigations over marriage situations harassed the church, " yet until toward the close of the eighteenth century, the church refused to yield to any demand for a re-examination of its rules." [74] In those days, if someone married the brother or sister of a dead spouse, much less a divorced one, the immediate result was excommunication. The development between those first days and the present time is marked by rigidity and controversy.

The earliest reference to remarriage in the records of the denomination was in the case of a Mr. Van Vleck in 1712. This gentleman was a Presbyterian minister. He had married again after the death of his wife. At a meeting of the Presbytery of Philadelphia at that time, Mr. Van Vleck was required to stop officiating as a minister until he could prove that his first wife was indeed dead. [75] This example may seem trivial and rather comical, but it reflects the times. It suggests the climate of confusion and concern in the days before the Revolution and during the Great Awakening.

The next date in which any records are found concerning remarriage is 1853. The law concerning marriage after divorce was passed at the General Assembly of that year and read as follows:

> Adultery and fornication committed after a contract being detected before marriage giveth justification for the innocent party to dissolve the contract. In the case of adultery after marriage, it is lawful for the innocent party to sue out a divorce, after the divorce to marry another, as if the offending party were dead.

> Although the corruption of man be such as to study
> arguments unduly to put asunder those whom God hath
> joined in marriage, yet nothing but adultery or such
> wilful desertion as can no way be remedied by the church
> and civil magistrates gives cause sufficient to the dis-
> solving the bond of marriage.[76]

This statement showed specifically what was considered legitimate in divorce and remarriage. It should be
added that nothing was left to individual desires. Persons
who had grounds for divorce were to follow an orderly
procedure in getting it, and not be left to "discretion in
their own cases." [77]

These grounds for divorce were considered Scriptural
and definite. The mere affirmation of them indicates discussion about remarriage. Yet, to remarry on any other
grounds brought dire results. A Midwestern minister, Mr.
Shields, learned this, to his sorrow.

In 1858, the General Assembly upheld a presbytery decision that charged Mr. Shields with adultery for marrying a second wife during the life of the first. The basis
of the decision was that Mr. Shields "had obtained a divorce in the civil court, in the judgment of the Presbytery, on other than Scriptural grounds." The result? Excommunication! [78]

In regard to second marriages, the minutes of the 1881
General Assembly record a lengthy and hot statement
against bigamy. The spirit of polygamy and bigamy was
held to be hostile to the "law of Christianity, the instinct
of morality and the essential principles of civilization and
to the existence of liberty for the people." [79]

From 1881 until 1926, there was no significant statement on the subject. In 1926, the General Assembly appointed a special commission to study remarriage. The

report of this special commission was presented in 1928. The General Assembly then voted to produce a stricter view of remarriage than before. This vote struck out of the law permission for divorce when there was " such wilful desertion as can no way be remedied by the church or civil magistrate." [80] This meant that adultery was the only basis.

In the Presbyterian Church, before a ruling by the General Assembly (an annual national assembly of the church) can have the force of constitutional law, it must be approved by a majority of the presbyteries and reapproved by the following General Assembly. Hence, it did not take long to get reaction to this new statement. With it, a chain reaction of General Assembly-presbytery argument was started that has not died yet. A presbytery, in a strongly worded overture, not only voted against the new ruling but requested a study of the whole divorce and remarriage laws. [81]

The commission to study this topic was appointed, and in 1930, under Dr. Ralph Marshall Davis, it presented a definition of marriage which is still held in high regard: [82]

Marriage is an institution ordained of God for the honor and happiness of mankind in which one man and one woman enter into a bodily and spiritual union pledging each to the other mutual love, honor, fidelity, forebearance, and comradeship such as should insure an unbroken continuance of their wedlock so long as both shall live. This institution finds its primary justification in the establishment and maintenance of the Christian home in which children shall be born and nurtured in the Christian faith.

On the side of civil government, the church recognizes marriage as a legal contract involving moral obligations of Christian citizenship.

With regard to divorce, the report defined the death of a marriage as both physical and spiritual:

> Beyond the fact that the marriage relation is terminated by death is the further fact that it may be destroyed by either party to the agreement proving unfaithful to the vows taken. That unfaithfulness may be found in the act of infidelity or irremediable desertion. Anything that kills love and deals death to the spirit of the union is infidelity.[83]

With regard to this type of spiritual death within a marriage, the report went on to hold that God does not deny free will in the marriage relationship. Therefore, the Commission held that God would never insist that a man and woman had to remain in the marriage relationship where the other spurned his or her love.

The Commission based its argument for this " spiritual " understanding of adultery on the fact that Paul himself added desertion. The Commission recognized the statements of Jesus. Yet, the conclusion was that Paul would never have allowed remarriage after separation " had the apostle understood our Lord's teaching to have a literal and universal application." [84] In the light of this understanding of adultery and desertion, the Commission concluded that there was no reason to change the existing standards.

With regard to the remarriage of divorced persons, the report built upon the Commission's study of divorce. The remarriage could take place only for the innocent party of a divorce based on the grounds stated. In addition, the marriage had to be " in the Lord."

This report was accepted by the Assembly. At its own request, the Commission was allowed to continue and make a further report the following year. In recognition of the concern that was gripping the church, the title of the new statement was changed from "Marriage and Divorce" to "Marriage, Divorce, and Remarriage."

There then followed one of the finest statements and studies of the subject ever done by the Presbyterian Church. It ranks with that of the Lutheran Church of the same year. The study enlarged upon the previous one, spoke of the place of children in divorce and remarriage, discussed the causes of divorce, and made a beginning report on the role of education. Under the sponsorship of the Commission, a book was published entitled *Twenty-four Views of Marriage*. This book represented every point of view on the subject. Even so liberal a thinker as Bertrand Russell was author of a chapter.

If, after this description of all the work and labor of this Commission, it is a blow to learn that the entire report was virtually rejected by the Assembly, think how the members of the Commission must have felt!

For the next twenty years, the General Assembly in particular, and the denomination in general, kept silent on this issue. Some persons may have been helped by the report, but the official law remained the same. Finally, in 1949, concern was expressed by presbyteries all over the country. A committee was again formed, and its report came in 1950.

Under the chairmanship of Rev. Albert G. Butzer, this committee confined itself strictly to the interpretation of the "problem" phrases in the law and machinery for carrying out the law. If the memory of what happened in 1931 still lingered, it is easy to understand why the committee took this limited approach.

Basically, the 1950 report did three things: it set up an application procedure for remarriage cases; it kept adultery and willful desertion as the bases for granting a divorce and performing a remarriage; and it required each presbytery to set up a commission on Christianity and marriage.[85] The report centered on Sec. 10 of Ch. XIV of the Directory for Worship. It required ministers to have all applicants for remarriage fill out a form. The marriage was to be solemnized for the innocent party only, and it was to be recorded with the presbytery.

The importance of this shift was to place the control of the remarriage situation, not in the hands of the minister, but in the hands of presbytery. "As will be readily observed," the report read, "these proposed changes will bring the whole matter of the remarriage of divorced persons definitely and directly under the control of presbytery, where we are convinced it belongs." [86]

The report was approved by the General Assembly. The presbyteries rejected it. Hence, the pattern of action and reaction continued.

In 1951, the committee rewrote its report and presented it to the General Assembly of 1951 in two parts. Overture A was approved and its substance is found in Section 10 of the present law. Overture B consisted of four paragraphs. The first called for a committee on Christian marriage in each presbytery, to which ministers might refer for aid. The second held that a decision by the presbytery committee was binding on the minister. The third and fourth paragraphs concerned Christian comity and the one-year waiting period.

Overture B was rejected. Since the last two paragraphs were reinstated the following year, it is clear that the denomination felt that full responsibility should rest in the hands of the minister.

From the standpoint of "realized forgiveness," the new Presbyterian law has great strength in that it recognizes the impossibility of defining an "innocent party." Further, as with the Lutheran law, it clearly recognizes the need for awareness of one's guilt. Also from the standpoint of "realized forgiveness," it must be observed that the committees of 1930 and 1950–1951 had far greater insight into the real issues at hand than is indicated by the legislation that survived their reports. But in view of the real problem involved in readiness for marriage, the present law has three glaring weaknesses.

Initially, it is negative and gives no basic guide as to what makes one ready to remarry. The old law may have been poorly used, but it had the virtue of trying to give the minister a guide as to what was involved. From the study of pastoral care, we know that it is not so much a sense of penitence that is needed as a sense of forgiveness.

In addition, the law is highly individualistic. By the very rejection of the participating role of the presbytery, the law was made this way. As such, it does not seem aware of the community or corporate dimension that was noted with Calvin. Nor is there any recognition of the place of the couple. The law is geared to the minister. The power and the responsibility are in his hands. Review comes only if *he* wants it. By leaving him alone, and not giving an adequate guide as to what makes for "readiness to marry," the law has actually increased his problem rather than helped it.

Finally, the law reflects no awareness of a Christian view of time. There is a reference to the need for spiritual compatibility. This would lead one to hope that a concept of fulfillment was in the making. To the contrary, the law goes on to say that this compatibility is important for the sake of children. This is cause-effect reasoning. If something happens now, it will result in something else then.

There is truth in this position, but it completely misses the Christian concept of time. References to a "three-day notice" and "one year" so as not to be hasty are based on an Old Testament view and do not suggest the Christian concept.

Although I would not say that the laws of the various denominations are good, neither could anyone condemn them as all bad. The laws are uneven. In understanding some of the dynamics involved in remarriage, the Lutheran law seems to be ahead of all the others. In being aware of the corporate nature of experience, the Episcopal Church takes the lead. Yet, no one of the denominational laws shows full awareness of the community experience or of the personal dynamics of the remarriage question. As a result, instead of helping, the laws are potentially dangerous. Why is this so? Consider the following:

The historical changes in the various denominational laws show that none of them have taken seriously the Christian concept of time as fulfillment or fullness (kairos).

There is no overt statement that proves this point. Nevertheless, the fate of some of the reports that did have it, the emphasis of other reports on a certain length of time, and the attitude of many pastors who have been interviewed support the statement. Across the denominations, there seems to have been a common factor. That factor was awareness of the unsatisfactory legalisms that had surrounded the divorce laws. With the exception of the Methodist law, no one of the four denominations represented has maintained the "adultery," "desertion," or "innocency" phrases. And the Methodist law has so expanded the meaning of those words as to deny a literal interpretation of them.

However, even the reports themselves give no evidence of awareness of the Christian view of time. The 1930 reports of the Presbyterian Church came close to it when they mentioned the needs for spiritual interpretation, awareness of the lessons of psychology, and awareness of the implications of theology. The Episcopal law also speaks of the spiritual factor in remarriage. And the need for proper instruction by the clergy is mentioned in Episcopalian literature. The Lutheran statement also lays great emphasis on the importance of education and the spiritual relationship.

If these comments about education and spiritual factors were amplified in terms of maturity and fulfillment, then we could say that the Christian view of time was in evidence. Such is not the case. In each instance, education is seen strictly as a matter of giving information. The accumulation of facts, through lectures, sermons, and books, it is hoped, will cause the problems of divorce to be solved. Here, there is no recognition that the issue in remarriage is not a question of intellectual awareness but of personal (emotional, intellectual, and spiritual) readiness.

In the same way, it is assumed in the Episcopal canon and the Presbyterian law that all a minister has to do is give a written statement of the "facts in the case" to the bishop or presbytery. If these "facts" were to include more than the legal status involved, there might be a basis for enthusiasm. There is nothing to indicate that that is the case.

The history of the denominations has shown a failure, as a whole, to recognize in their legitimate interdependence the corporate and the individual aspects of remarriage.

The study of actual pastoral interviews showed three

things: Each person in the interview was an individual in his own right. Each person in the interview was part of one whole experience that bound the three of them together. Each group of individuals was related to some community — church, family, and local society.

As a loyal Presbyterian, I can point to places where the sense of community and awareness of the individual have not been lost in the church law. Loyal Episcopalians, loyal Lutherans, and loyal Methodists can do the same for their own laws. But how do these laws measure up if one takes seriously the necessity of realized forgiveness? For all that can be said in favor of the laws, it must also be said that they have failed to recognize the place of the individual and of the corporate dimension of life at a basic level. There is nothing in the modern laws comparable with this awareness in the Geneva statements.

Attention has just been called to the way in which education is seen primarily on an intellectual basis. The place of the group experience in educational growth is ignored. The evidence par excellence is in the motive that has forced much of the recent discussion of divorce and remarriage regulations. The Presbyterian situation is the most familiar to me, but conversations with fellow pastors in the Lutheran and Episcopal churches make it clear that my denomination is not unique in this example.

Rather than stating the underlying dynamics of the individual, and the meaning of an individual life in the presence of the church, the 1950 Presbyterian reports sought only " clarification." To say that a matter of procedure is clarified is no guarantee that the procedure was good in the first place. It in no way means that the real issues were understood. The dominance of this pragmatic motive is seen in the reasons for raising the concern about remarriage at all. One overture to the General Assembly which called for the committee formation and the subsequent Presbyterian law said, in part:

> The Presbytery . . . feels the conviction that there is need for more exact and specific definition of the position of the Church on the remarriage of divorced persons. We believe that throughout the entire Church our ministers are desiring precise and clear definition of rights, limitations, duties, in this function of the ministry. We believe that the confusion and varying standards of our clergy in their discretionary interpretation of our stands in this vital matter is neither satisfactory to them, conducive to the good, or contributory to the good name and honor of the Church.
>
> Therefore, the Presbytery . . . overtures the General Assembly to create and establish a commission or committee . . . to give clear and more definite guidance . . . where the offices of the Church may be requested in the remarriage of divorced persons.[87]

This overture was quite correct in its appraisal of the situation. Ministers were desiring a precise definition. The clergy did want " definite guidance." The supreme evidence for this is that the Commission's report was rejected for one reason, viz., " impractical."

From a pastoral standpoint, the necessity of real forgiveness and, from the Reformer's standpoint, the necessity of corporateness mean that such a " blueprint " is impossible. The most dynamic interpretation of law means that the rules must give the guiding principles and the framework in which the problem may be met. Because no two people are alike, the law can give guidance, but it cannot define every situation.

Because of this emphasis on the practical, it is not surprising that the final laws have contained nothing about realized forgiveness. On the contrary, the charge must be made that *the laws allow for a false sense of forgiveness.* They allow a person to be married on a subjectively interpreted reading of the law by one man. They allow a person to be married on a detached decision by an official, or committee that can look only at the legal evidence. Either way, the couple have the feeling that all is well because of the official blessing from the church. The fact is that neither the desire of the couple, the subjective decision of the minister, nor the official act of a disinterested group may bear any resemblance to a genuine " readiness for marriage." Unless the laws point to the necessity of realized forgiveness in the couple, the minister, and the church as a whole, they do not speak to the real question.

The final evidence that the laws do not help with regard to the basic issue in remarriage is that they have not initially been concerned with the real issue. This may seem harsh; for, indeed, many ministers and many of the commissions have been deeply concerned. This is a criticism not so much of the persons who have wrestled with the laws as of the denominations in their altering the recommendations of those concerned. It is a criticism for which every one of us who is a pastor, every one who is a church officer, every one who is a part of the church stands under judgment. For the fact is that no question for interpretation of the law or the canon has ever arisen out of concern for the couple involved in divorce. *History documents the fact that the concern of the churches about divorce in America has arisen from a cultural reaction to the position of the church.*

The fact that the laws may help clarify matters for the minister and protect the " purity of the church " in the face of cultural pressures may be true. That, however, does not make the law relevant to the remarriage situation itself. On the contrary, if the laws have emerged in the reaction to cultural pressure, any relevance to remarriage itself would seem impossible. To have a law that is relevant to both cultural pressure and the remarriage of divorced persons would be purely coincidence.

The basis for this charge against those of us in the church is this: the shifting views on remarriage parallel changes in cultural viewpoints and are often in reaction to those viewpoints. Consider the facts: In its early history, the Presbyterian Church reacted to the presence of infidelity and a philosophy known as deism. Dr. Trinterud points out that the challenge of infidelity and deism, and the need to counteract them, was the one clear need that the church saw in the years following the Revolutionary War.[88]

There was quite a struggle, and, as often happens, the " enemy " in part conquered the church. Dr. Trinterud points out that " the pressure of infidelity and deism stirred up an abnormal interest in theological polemic. . . . Greater and greater reliance was, therefore, placed upon the ' system of sound doctrine ' as the only infallible guard against the new irreligion of the day." [89] This meant that intellectual factors became dominant and that full account was not taken of the emotional life. Hence, the result was seen in the very legal interpretation of the divorce and remarriage situation when a minister had to prove that his previous wife was dead.

The same type of example is seen in the mid-nineteenth century. The Episcopal Church decided to abide by the rules in England until such time as they could work on the matter themselves. Why, then, did they never get around

to it until 1868? Is it just coincidence that it was not until
the same year that the Presbyterian Church really took up
the issue again after its colonial formulation of the law?
The factor common to both denominations was the end of
the War Between the States. It is almost expected that
after every war there is an increase in the divorce rate.
During and after the war, immorality was on the upswing.
With more immorality there came more illegitimate births.
With illegitimate babies there came the horror of infanticide — the killing of children at birth. As a clear indication
that its statement of the law was in reaction to infanticide,
the Presbyterian regulation spoke of it directly.[90]

Another "coincidence" centers on the dates 1877 and
1879. For the Episcopal Church, the next major statement
concerning remarriage came in 1877. For the Presbyterians
it came two years later. Why? Following on the heels of the
Civil War, there came, in the third quarter of the nine-
teenth century, a reaction to Mormonism. The Church of
Jesus Christ of Latter-day Saints began with the revelation
to Joseph Smith in New York early in the century. It was
forced to move westward. Finally, in Utah, Mormons became established as a growing and powerful group. The
emphasis in the Episcopal law with regard to a man's marrying a woman, "the first wife still living," was a reflection
of the concern over bigamy. The Presbyterians ruled that
bigamists were to be excluded from the church.[91] Mr.
Shields, as we have already seen, was called a bigamist because he did not divorce his first wife for adultery or desertion.

The greatest "coincidences" are the recent ones. Why
is it that the Episcopal, Lutheran, and Presbyterian denominations all picked 1930–1931 as the time for the most
elaborate discussions of remarriage since the colonies?

Why is it that these same denominations made no significant changes for the next twenty years? Why is it that these groups picked the 1950's for their latest major revisions? By what coincidence did these three remove "adultery," "desertion," and "innocency" clauses at the same time?

The common denominator in the thirties was the depression superimposed upon the "roaring twenties." In the presence of that, some groups, as shown above, wanted strict statements about divorce and remarriage. In these years, there was a growing reaction to social insecurity. Thus, within the studies of the Lutheran and Presbyterian groups, there was also a move in a social direction. Some were trying to meet the problem through social understanding. Others were resorting to increased reliance on laws. Both are examples of reaction to the times of which the issue of remarriage was a part.

In the late forties, there was again the common denominator of the war. In addition, a great deal of unsolicited publicity hit the Presbyterian Church. In Florida, there was the marriage of Bobo Rockefeller; and in Los Angeles a Presbyterian minister married two movie personalities with divorce records. The great uproar that grew out of these marriages — particularly the one in California — was reflected in the desire of the Los Angeles Presbytery to have clarification of procedures.

The fact that past debates about the remarriage of divorced persons usually arose in coincidence with some great cultural move leads to just one conclusion. The views of the churches on remarriage have been guided by cultural reactions. It cannot be proven, but it seems reasonable to hold that none of the decisions made by the American churches have been made with much understanding of these cultural pressures. Surely, the awareness has not been sufficient enough for the decisions to be free and objective.

This is another way of saying that the denominations themselves have not experienced realized forgiveness in relation to their culture and its past. The denominations have not been able to deal effectively with what the Lutherans observed to be the church's part in the failure. The church has felt only guilt in regard to events that have surrounded it and in regard to the actions of some of its ministers. By producing the laws, the denominations have given *themselves* a false sense of forgiveness. It is false simply because the questions asked were in relation to the pressure of the guilt or the culture and not in relation to the issue of remarriage itself.

In turning to the reason for the lack of awareness about the corporate-individual relationship in remarriage matters, Dr. James H. Nichols has given a clue in his emphasis on the place of pietism in the United States. He stated that what Troeltsch had called "ascetic Protestantism" had had, of all Christian traditions, the most extensive influence in Western life in the last three hundred years. This influence permeated the political life of our country and has been seen in the developing individualism of the American scene.

Dr. Nichols says that pietism is characterized by an ignoring of general structure and a building of small fellowships within the structure. These characteristics have shown up in the discussion about marriage laws. Both the Lutheran and the Presbyterian groups have shown a desire for rules. Yet, particularly in the Presbyterian, there was a reaction against anything that was not simple and pat. Further, the elimination in all groups of the words

" adultery," " desertion," and " innocence " is partly a reflection of a shift away from structure. As one man wrote, " I just ask the couple if they love each other."

At the same time, it must be noted that there have been significant groups in the denominations that have shown awareness of the broad scope of the remarriage issue. The Episcopal and Presbyterian denominations have started research in this area. The Lutheran Church has done some significant study. The Family Life Research group of the Presbyterian Church has done some fundamental research on the whole nature of the Christian family.

In effect, the changes in the remarriage laws have sometimes served to shift or settle responsibility for remarriage, but they have not solved the problem.

The question of time is not understood in a Christian sense. Also, the rules speak to the issues of the culture more than to the problem at hand; yet there is no recognition of the influence of culture in this development. As a result, the interpretation of the actual laws are either legalistic or unjustifiably subjective. There is no proper awareness of the relationship between the community and the individual. As a result, there is no realized forgiveness provided for in the laws as they now stand.

Within the denominations, there are significant movements that show a growing awareness of these weaknesses. It is to be hoped that these groups will have the opportunity to bring their understanding to bear on a reworking of the laws and the approach of the denominations to remarriage.

7

THE MINISTER'S PROCEDURE
IN A MEANINGFUL MARRIAGE

A meaningful marriage needs two things. It needs the realization of forgiveness. It needs an adequate means of expressing this forgiveness.

The importance of forgiveness has already been discussed. The failure of church law at this point has now been presented. From start to finish, what, then, does make for a meaningful marriage? Nothing can guarantee the future; but what can be done so that, when the service is over, all can say, " This marriage was real "?

In relation to the remarriage of divorced persons, the minister's role as the " common ground " in the presence of which the couple operate has already been mentioned. This role has two parts. In one sense, the minister is the prophet. He is the individual who tries to help the couple come to discover the will of God for themselves. He is the " forthteller." In another sense, the minister is the priest. He represents the Christian community and through him the universal church. He is the one who will say what the law is. He will state the context in which the couple will come to be married. It is in the " two in one " personality that every minister acts.

For convenience, the procedure with regard to the remarriage of a divorced person can be divided into three sections. It is in the course of this procedure that the realization of forgiveness becomes clear and is expressed.

First comes the inquiry. This is usually a phone call. Here, the minister's position as "priest" is uppermost. The central question of the voice on the other end of the phone is, "Will you marry us?" Closely related is the question, "What must we do?"

From the outset, a different mood surrounds the marriage of a divorced person from that of a nondivorced person. With the latter, there is usually excitement mixed with questioning. Few people ever doubt that a minister will officiate at the marriage. But in every instance of a divorce and remarriage — even a divorce of twenty years' standing — there is a cloud. Emotional responses run all the way from defensiveness and cocksureness to being just plain scared. Because of this, a minister often comes to feel that he can recognize the presence of a divorce long before anyone has mentioned the subject.

MINISTER: Is there a divorce involved?
PARISHIONER: Well, yes, but he turned around and married someone else the day after the divorce.

Or:

M: I would like for you to come and talk before we make any definite plans.
P: Well, fine. Uh, I should tell you that my fiancé has been divorced.
M: I see.
P: But I've even seen the other woman, and really, it shouldn't make any difference.

The second step is the interview. Here, the minister is

primarily the "prophet." This may be a series of interviews. It may be no more than an interview with the
couple together. It may be an interview with the individuals separately. (There are ministers who will marry a
couple on the strength of the telephone conversation. Such
a procedure is rare, however. Even the most casual minister usually will have a discussion in which he can at least
look at the marriage license.)

As the prophet in this relationship, the minister or
church board must have a working awareness of the Holy
Spirit. In many of the interviews in this book, the minister
had a basic principle: viz., the Holy Spirit was operating
in the situation and had to be free to govern. It is this
awareness that differentiates the Christian from the non-
Christian marriage counselor.

This means that the minister sees his role as one of
creating the type of situation in which the right decision
can be evolved. He is not sitting as a great authority to
pronounce judgment. This view follows from the discovery
that the minister is not the only individual in the making
of the decision. In practice, this truth will express itself in
many ways. At one point in his interview with Dorie, it
will be recalled that the minister said: "I didn't quite get
that. You say it would help him or you?" Dorie had made
a statement. The minister missed its significance entirely.
Therefore he said so. Such a statement means, by implication: I'm human too; I didn't understand. We are in this
together; will you help me out? Or, at another spot, after
a statement by Dorie, the minister said the following:

MINISTER: But now is it possible to suggest this — that you
    have first dreamed up other ideas of what marriage is,
    to which you are then trying to conform instead of
    thinking of marriage in terms of being a need where

both of you need each other, both give to each other
or meet the need the other has? Is it possible that you
are dreaming up a picture about marriage that you're
trying to conform to, and isn't it also possible that marriages are all of different types? Each one has to be
created anew.

To this, Dorie replied, " That's very wise."

This interview had seen real involvement on the part of
Dorie and the minister. At this point, the pastor self-con-
sciously chose to pull together what he felt logically grew
out of the interview. Intellectually, his analysis had some
merit. She did have an idea about marriage that was not
fully realistic. Nevertheless, this speech accomplished
nothing for Dorie. In fact, it shifted her attention from
what had been her concern. Her comment, " That's very
wise," was almost the perfect squelch. After all, the quickest
way to quiet a minister is to agree with him. When a minister talks too much, he will often get this squelch. He will
indeed be wise if he watches for it.

In this interview, the minister did watch. He picked up
the cue from what Dorie said. In his next comment, he
moved back to her real situation by saying, " You are saying, then, that you want the marriage to develop out of
what you both have to offer, is that it? " Dorie then took
the lead and went on. Had the minister not fully believed
in the activity of the Spirit, he would probably have continued to be the authority making wise statements.

Humanists would disagree that the Holy Spirit is active.
They would argue that the individual has the inner re-
sources necessary for the solving of the problem. To them,
the counselor creates the atmosphere that lets these re-
sources come to light.

Whether it is the inner resource or the Holy Spirit is

not our problem. Both humanist and minister would agree that a power other than themselves is operative. As Christians, we understand this power to be the Holy Spirit. The question ministers must continually ask as they counsel is, "Am I taking seriously my presence or the Spirit's presence?"

This mood is reflected by the minister's letting the parishioner consistently have the "right of way" in talking. He consistently acts on the basis that the interview belongs to the parishioner and his or her problems, not to him and his reactions.

Within this view of the Holy Spirit, however, the general interview procedure may differ from minister to minister. Some pastors are quite directive. They have a list of questions; they ask these and get answers. Others are nondirective. Still others have an approach that seems a combination of the two. A number of ministers in very large congregations (over two thousand) report that they listen for the first forty minutes. In the last twenty, they then give their appraisal of the situation and their decision. The couple are then free to do what they want with that decision.

Other ministers rely heavily on questionnaires that have been formed by Rev. Granger Wesberg, of the University of Chicago, by Duke University in North Carolina, or by magazines such as the *Ladies' Home Journal* and *McCall's*. A Rochester minister stated that he once gave a questionnaire to every couple that came to him. Now he uses it selectively; but, from experience with it, he asks the questions that he uses in the course of discussion.

It is possible for a directive minister to conduct his interviews in a way consistent with a belief in the presence of the Holy Spirit. Talks with those who are directive, however, leads one to question how many of them have seriously considered the implications of their procedure for their doctrine of the Holy Spirit — or the reverse. Those with a directive approach tend to be authoritarian. Those with a nondirective approach tend to miss their responsibility for setting the limits within which the interviews will take place. The one forgets the true concept of prophet; the other forgets the role of priest.

If the dangers are recognized, I personally favor the nondirective approach. It has three assumptions. One is that the parishioner has certain thoughts and feelings which he or she must assimilate in order to have a successful marriage. A second is that the source for this assimilation is in the person, not in the minister. A third is that the parishioner must reach his own conclusion within the structural framework that the minister sets. Sometimes the minister must make a decision. The point is that this procedure allows for the times when the couple will also make a decision.

The differences in approach by various people do not change the fact of the dynamic experience that is in the interview situation. Even within the same approach, the dynamic factors will be different for each different person. To be remembered is the fact that, regardless of the approach, realized forgiveness must take place.

The final stage in the remarriage of a divorced person is the marriage ceremony and all that surrounds it. Here, the minister is both prophet and priest at the same time. He is priest in the sense that he is the authority who performs the ceremony. He is prophet in the sense that he is the unifying symbol of what is taking place. In him, as it were, are represented the concerns of the church, the society, the couple, and the families.

To make forgiveness real, there must be a means of giving it expression. That which surrounds the marriage ceremony plays this function. What is it that adequately symbolizes the reality of forgiveness? The answer to that question will depend on the person and his culture.

For the person of Roman Catholic culture, it will mean some sort of concrete form of absolution that indicates admittance to the Sacrament. To the Orthodox Jew, it will mean the literal emptying of one's pockets into a flowing body of water to carry away all guilt. To those who live within the general free-church framework, it may be as simple as a statement from the pastor saying, " I will agree to remarry you." When this statement is made and accepted in the full knowledge of what the minister represents, there comes the awareness that the forgiveness is real.

The use of the sacrament of Communion in connection with marriage ought to be considered here. Protestants generally object to Communion in connection with a marriage. They feel that it looks too much like the Catholic Mass. Legitimately, they resent the thought that there is something magical in the idea of Communion offered to the couple. In this resentment, however, Protestants have overlooked the value that the sacrament of Communion has within it for those who are about to remarry. If it is correct to emphasize that church discipline is for maintaining the purity of the church and the Lord's Supper, then Communion has a vital part to play in the remarriage of divorced persons.

In most churches, Communion cannot be served at the whim of the minister. It can be served only upon the approval of some powers beyond the minister — the bishop, the presbytery, the board of deacons. This is so because the Sacrament is never done in any name other than the name of God. To receive it implies something about the relationship between man and his God. In and of itself, the Sacrament is a symbol of the real forgiveness of God. The necessity of agreement by the church in letting one take the Sacrament is a symbol of real forgiveness by the community of the faithful. The observation of the sacrament of Communion prior to the marriage service (not afterward, as in the Mass) is a powerful expression of the reality of forgiveness. Particularly if this is observed with the participation of the entire congregation, I can think of nothing that would make the fullness of forgiveness the more real to a couple about to be married.

In remarriage, however, more than just forgiveness must become real. The reality of a new "one flesh" must become real. There must be a "new creation." The act of sexual intercourse suggests this one flesh on a physical plane. There are also mental exchanges in which two people enter into the experiences of each other and become one. Finally, on the spiritual level, the marriage ceremony itself gives expression to the one flesh, the interpersonal person, the new creation, within the presence of God. Yet, this will not happen if the symbols of the marriage ceremony are not the symbols of the couple involved and of the minister. If the man does not believe in Jesus Christ, it makes no sense to marry a couple in the name of Christ. This is true no matter how much the girl wants a " church wedding."

The instance of Robert and Nancy is typical of a minister's attempt to help make the marriage ceremony an expression of not only the realized forgiveness but also the new person that was being created.

Robert had been married, but the marriage was annulled because certain laws had been violated in the marriage process. This first marriage had taken place ten years prior to the interview. The minister had several sessions with Robert and one with Nancy. The minister had come to the conclusion that Robert's first marriage was definitely a thing of the past, but Robert had concerns that did need investigation. The place of sex and the problem of income were matters that needed discussion. For Nancy, there was the necessity of discussing the Reformed tradition as such. When the time came to talk about the ceremony itself, the decision to marry had been made.

The minister explained that the service would open with a statement to the congregation as a whole. This statement would recognize the corporate aspect of the marriage. When the minister asks if anyone knows of any reason why the two should not be married, the silence serves as a congregational blessing on what is about to take place. The minister then explained that the second part would be a specific charge to the couple. The purpose of this charge would be to focus attention on their responsibility as a couple and as individuals standing in the presence of God.

It is perhaps the discussion pertaining to the wedding vows that best illustrates how the principles of the previous chapters apply even in the discussion of the marriage liturgy. The excerpt from this discussion with Robert and Nancy is as follows:

MINISTER: Now, there are several forms of the vows that you may use. After you have decided, I will write them out for you. If you would like to say them from memory, I think you would find it meaningful. Either way, I wish you would memorize them so that you really know what it is you are going to say. As I have stated before, you are marrying each other; I am not marrying you. These are the vows. (*The minister read two familiar vows.*)

ROBERT: I like the last one.

M: That is the historic one.

NANCY: And I'd like to memorize them.

M: I see. (*Pause.*) You really feel that is the one you like?

R: Well, somehow, that expresses what I think we're saying. It is the one I was brought up with, too.

N: Yes. Somehow, I don't know, it seems more like the thing you've looked forward to.

M: And then we come to the ring. There are two suggested statements on the ring too. (*The minister read these.*)

R: What was the first one again?

M: (*The minister repeated it.*)

R: I like that one.

N: That's fine with me too.

Usually, in discussion of the service itself, ministers do not pursue feelings as much as they might. It should be remembered that the worship service is full of symbols that could raise doubts and concern. There may be fear on the part of the couple to question the meaning, not to mention the procedure, of the marriage service. After a divorce, another couple may feel concern about the phrase, "Whom God hath joined together, let no man put asunder." Free discussion of this phrase and the emotions that surround it will often have direct bearing on a person's awareness of guilt and forgiveness. Different parts of the service will have different meanings in each instance, and these meanings must not be overlooked.

Some of these errors, or missed feelings, were evident in the discussion with Robert and Nancy. Nevertheless,

the I-thou relationship was real. There was a mutual concern for feelings. The pastor consistently gave openings
for discussion of what was being said. The rapport shown
by the ease with which each of the three picked up the
conversation, yet without interrupting, suggested I-thou
relationships. The experience of a new creation was becoming real. The reality of the new creation was the basis or
ground for further experiences of the I-thou relationship.
The full actualization of this ground in the presence of which
the couple can experience the I-thou relationship may come
after the ceremony, or it may come within the ceremony, or
it may come before the ceremony. The potential for it was
confirmed before and in this interview.

Note, in these conversations, the part played by the minister as priest. Certain things were " given " which the
Christian community needed in order to symbolize what
would take place. Even the couple needed this. By asking
the minister to suggest the service, the two were, in effect,
asking him to provide the symbols that would make their
relationship communicable. The function of helping people speak to others — particularly God — is the work of a
priest. However, it is the necessity of making symbols real
to the people involved that has required the Reformation
position also to insist on both the preaching and hearing
of the word of God in any true service of worship. In the
sermon, the minister presents an interpretation of Scripture so that, by means of it, God's word can become real
to the worshiper. Such is the evidence of the presence of
the church. When he does this, the minister is a prophet.

This point is supremely true at the marriage ceremony.
There must be that part of the ceremony in which the minister tries to pull together the experience of the community and the people and the couple, so that the *kairos* event

can be the experience of that moment. This is another way of saying that, even in the marriage ceremony, the place of the minister as prophet is not lost in his responsibility as priest. It is for him to create that type of situation in which the new creation, the *kairos* moment, may be experienced as real.

To see how this approach was finally exemplified in the marriage service, a few passages from that service are in order. The minister began by quoting from a psalm: "Except the Lord build the house, they labor in vain that build it." Addressing the congregation as a whole, he went on to say:

Dearly beloved, we are assembled in the presence of God to unite this man and this woman in holy marriage, which is ordained of God, regulated by his commandments, blessed by our Lord, Jesus Christ, and to be held in honor amongst all men. Let us therefore reverently attend unto the words of the institution of this sacred estate:

Marriage was ordained of God in Eden, and confirmed in Cana of Galilee by the gracious presence and miraculous blessing of our Lord, Jesus Christ. It is to unite one man and one woman as long as they both shall live. It is written, "Honor thy father and thy mother." Our Lord has said, "For this cause shall a man leave father and mother and cleave only to his wife, and these two shall be one flesh." So also ought a wife be unto her husband.

For as much as these two have come here to be made one in marriage, if there be any here present who know of any just cause why they should not be joined in this holy estate, I require him now make it known, or ever after to hold his peace.

Let us pray.

Eternal God, through thy love, we have come to know thee as "our Father." So look upon us in these moments that what we say and do may be in accord with thy will.

As by thy providence, thou hast led the lives of these two until this moment, so by thy grace may they experience thy presence at this moment. May there be such an awareness of thy love and forgiveness that they may put in the past what is in the past, and that they may move forward through this time, this day, and these years, in newness of life and strength of spirit. Through Jesus Christ, our Lord. Amen.

Speaking to the couple directly, the minister gave this short homily:

Inasmuch as you have come here to be married, I charge you now to remember, and ever to recall, what our Lord, through his apostles, has said to those who would come to the moment of marriage: that they should cherish a mutual esteem and love; that they should bear with each other's weaknesses and infirmities; that they should comfort each other in sickness, trouble, and sorrow; that they should provide for each other, and for their household, in temporal things; and that they should pray for and encourage each other in those things that pertain to God. May each of you always be able to say to the other, in the words of Holy Scripture: "Whither thou goest, I will go; and where thou lodgest, I will lodge: thy people shall be my people, and thy God, my God: . . . the Lord do so to me, and more also, if aught but death part thee and me."

Although the actual statement was slightly longer than given here, and was extemporaneous, these words were the essence of his meditation.

After the questions pertaining to the desire of the couple to marry, which are symbolic because they confirm the engagement and the decisions of the counseling sessions, the bride was " given away." The vows were then said as follows:

I, *Robert*, take thee, *Nancy*; To be my wedded wife; And I do promise and covenant; Before God and these witnesses; To be thy loving and faithful husband; In plenty and in want; In joy and in sorrow; In sickness and in health; As long as we both shall live.

I, *Robert*, take thee, I mean, I, *Nancy*, take thee, *Robert*; To be my wedded husband; And I do promise and covenant; Before God and these witnesses; To be thy loving and faithful wife; In plenty and in want; In joy and in sorrow; In sickness and in health; As long as we both shall live.

The service then followed the usual procedure of the exchanging of rings, the pastoral prayer, and the other liturgical forms as found in *The Book of Common Worship*.

Consider several aspects of what took place in this service. First, there was recognition of the part and place of culture in our daily living. The first words were addressed to the congregation, not to the couple. Secondly, in words both to the couple and to the congregation, there was recognition of the reality of God in all of life. Thirdly, in the prayer, there was recognition of the past and a symbolic placing of the past in the proper context within the experience of the couple. Fourthly, there was the symbolic creation of the one flesh that brings into actualization or open realization the interpersonal-person referred to in the counseling sessions. This came in the couple facing each other, and exchanging their pledges to each other, not to the minister. It represented the total giving of one to the other and the pledge of the total receiving of one by the other. (An added touch, in this particular service, came when Nancy slipped and began by saying, " I, Robert," instead of giving her own name. This was a mistake. Yet it was a part of her. It was accepted. Her correction equally was accepted, and she went on to repeat the vow.) Fifthly, the creation of this one flesh was then recognized by the minister's charge that no man should try to separate them. Finally, the benediction recognized the ongoing nature of this experience. As with the counseling, this occurred in the presence of the minister, whose function was to create the atmosphere or condition in the presence of which all these things could take place. It is clear here, and in Reformed theology, that the minister did not marry the couple. They married each other, and he merely officiated.

The worship in which the wedding took place, then, completed that which began with the first interview. The preparation for the performing of the ceremony brought everyone in the corporate area together. The service itself suggested the approval of the corporate. The service itself showed the dynamic relationship between the two individuals mediated by the minister in the presence of God. In the marriage ceremony, the experiences became expressed through the symbols of the marriage service. These words were the same that others had used. Yet, because these people were not the same as other couples, these words really symbolized different things for this couple. Here, a marriage had taken place.

8

A MEANINGFUL LAW

Throughout this book, we have looked at the remarriage of divorced people from various angles. We have seen it from the perspective of the pastor, the couple, and the church itself. We have seen it historically and we have seen it psychologically. We have spoken of the failure of a marriage to take place, and we have described a full marriage service. By way of summary and conclusion, it now falls to us to state what I call the preliminaries of remarriage: the conditions of remarriage and the law itself.

Whether a person is a church officer, the pastor, the couple involved, or just an interested observer, certain facts must be clear. These facts are central for understanding remarriage.

1. *Separation is a fact of life.* From the prophet Malachi to the most liberal member of the most liberal modern church, it is clear that separation is hated. It is evidence of the sin of the world. Still, it is real.

2. *Separation in marriage is a part of the basic split in all of creation.* Although many interpreters of the Reformers go no farther than this, most of them see the lessons of psychoanalysis as another way of describing this split in

163

people. As it grows out of the first sentence in Genesis and finds full expression in both Calvin and Luther, this fact holds to the fundamental oneness of all God's creation. This means that a problem in one segment cannot be considered as unrelated to the whole of life. A split in one marriage is related, therefore, to the whole of creation's need for God's grace.

3. *It is a fact that a marriage can die.*

4. *It is a fact that a remarriage is legitimate after the death of a spouse.*

5. *Therefore, remarriage should be allowed after a divorce.* This statement is a conclusion placed upon statements in the Bible and the writings of the Reformation. My argument is that not to recognize divorce is to deny the oneness of God's creation. It is to deny that what theology calls " the condition of sin " may have its effect in every area of life. To say that one hates divorce is not to say that divorce does not exist. A decision must still be made as to how to deal with that which does exist.

This statement is further based on the argument that a marriage may die spiritually, just as it may die physically. If remarriage can be granted upon physical death, then it must also be granted for spiritual death.

6. *It is a fact that there are several ways of understanding time.* In the Christian faith, the historical understanding of time is never denied. Important to us is the point that, in the Christian faith, time can be understood as more than history. It can be understood as " fullness " or fulfillment as well.

7. *The problem of the remarriage of divorced persons cannot be approached unilaterally.* Both from the experience of church history and from the experiences of individual ministers, this point has emerged: solutions to the

problem have been sought either in the area of personal tensions or in the area of corporate tensions. The case studies above show that these two cannot be separated in actual fact. The minister has to deal with the total picture of the man or the woman, and with personal problems, in the context of the corporate experience.

With these facts as the backdrop, what, then, are the conditions for remarriage?

The fundamental aim in remarriage, as also in a first marriage, is to become a genuinely " new creation." For the minister, this element may not be immediately clear; but the lack of integrity felt by the minister when he is trapped in a remarriage situation shows that this is as true for him as for the couple. The minister expresses his understanding and relationship to all of life by the dealings he has with people. This is equally, if not particularly, true in the matter of marriage counseling. It is a critical encounter in which he is able to bring to the fore his experience of " fullness " in relation to the church he serves, the faith he holds, and the people with whom he is confronted. His experience of salvation finds concrete expression in the integrity he maintains.

For the church, the remarriage situation is a matter of salvation as well as of integrity because in marriage the church has always seen the symbolic expression of the relation between God and his people. The true marriage has the function of coming to terms with a modern-day fellowship, on the one hand, and a great heritage of history on the other. From the days of the Old Testament, remarriage has been an example of the overcoming of the separation between man and God. The story of Hosea is a case in point. Yet, remarriage is not only an example, it is one of the means by which expression is actually given to the overcoming of that separation. This point is suggested by Paul when he said, about marital conduct, "As Christ loved the church, . . . so husbands should love their wives as their own bodies " (Eph. 5:25, 28).

Initially, this statement sounds as though the marriage relationship is just a parallel to the relation between Christ and the church. Yet, Paul then goes on to say: " For this reason a man shall leave his father and mother and be joined to his wife, and the two shall become one. This is a great mystery, and I take it to mean Christ and the church; however, let each one of you love his wife as himself " (Eph. 5:32-33). Here, the apostle is saying that the statement about forsaking parents must be understood both in relation to the church and to marriage. Thus, from the earliest history of the Christian church, there has been the understanding of marriage as an expression of the relationship between people and God. In so far as remarriage is a matter of overcoming a past sin and re-establishing a relationship of oneness, the expression of the atonement with God becomes even more striking in a second marriage than in the case of a first.

The culture can also find an integrity through the remarriage of a divorced person. From the interviews I have had with a few parents as well as with divorcees themselves, it seems fair to say that the original family of a divorced person generally approves a remarriage. The feeling often is, " Gosh, the first one was so unhappy, he really deserves a better break." Or, " She seems like a nice girl, and I'm glad to see this happening." Whether or not this feeling grows out of a sense of guilt for the cultural factors that are implied in bringing about a divorce, or from a sense of relief at getting a person " off my hands," or is just joy in another's happiness is hard to tell. Perhaps all are involved. The fact is, despite the sense of horror that is righteously expressed by many newspapers and church groups, interviews of individuals (even people within these very selfsame church groups) indicate a basic sense of " being glad " at a remarriage.

Finally, the remarriage conducted on the bases I have suggested is a source of fulfillment for the couple in expression of their integrity. The great majority of divorcees feel a lack of fulfillment after their divorce. Of these, 66 per cent actually do remarry. Of those who do remarry, 83 per cent never get divorced again. This does not say that 83 per cent actually feel a complete sense of fulfillment in a perfect marriage, but it is to suggest that these feel a greater sense of fulfillment in being remarried than in getting another divorce. Of the other 17 per cent, 9 per cent succeed only in a third remarriage, 1 per cent in a fourth, and 7 per cent never succeed.[92]

In a remarriage, the first condition appears to be the *desire for wholeness* and the experience of it. For this to take place, however, the evidence of the previous chapters suggests that certain other conditions are necessary.

To begin with, the *previous marriage must have died.* A person may die physically, and this death makes the experience clear for the survivor. The individual is dead, and the marriage is dead. As previously asserted, the spiritual death is just as real as the physical death — and just as important. Three fourths of all remarriages are of divorced persons. Whether divorced or widowed, the controlling factor is the reality of a spiritual death. The problem of releasing the person who has died means that people have not been able really to accept the spiritual aspect of the death of a marriage. The physical death of a person is one of the symbolic expressions of the death of a marriage. It is the conclusion of this study that the committing of adultery is another of the physical, symbolic expressions of the death of a marriage. The inability to realize the truth of the spiritual death results in some remarried people being psychological bigamists. Thus, a condition of remarriage is the complete death of a previous marriage, fully accepted into the awareness of the remarrying party, so that there is allowed the creation of one flesh.

Another condition is *the necessity for making an individual decision.* As shown, this individual decision has to be made by the man and the woman as well as by the minister. One cannot abdicate this responsibility either to the state or to the church. To do the first is to ignore the reality of a smaller society, the church, of which the minister and couple are a part. To do the second is to ignore the presence of the larger society in which we all are citizens. To do either is to deny the fact that, as members of both the larger and smaller societies (state and church), we are still responsible individuals. We must live with ourselves. Like it or not, we will carry the consequences of our decisions. Therefore, the minister's function is to act in his specific situation as the channel of God by creating that sort of framework in which he, the man, and the woman can come to the individual decision required of them.

The truth of this individual factor has its support in Calvin's view of the individual minister's task. It is further supported in any study of the dynamic experience where it is seen that, ultimately, a "yes" or "no" decision has to be made by one of the three parties; and this decision is conclusive. If any one of the three says "no," there is no remarriage.

Just as an individual decision has to be made because the individual is a real part of the picture, so a corporate decision must be made. The strongest lesson to be drawn from this study is that there is a corporate dimension to remarriage, and that this corporate dimension has been ignored or neglected in post-Reformation approaches to the remarriage of divorced persons. The state is a part of the corporate picture, and the prerogatives of the state cannot be taken over by the individual because that would mean a denial of the relation of the individual to the culture of society. The laws of the state may be changed as an expression of that culture; but taking of the law into one's own hands is to forget the existence of that culture. One does not meet dissatisfaction with a culture by acting as though it did not exist.

Just as truly, one cannot assume for himself the prerogatives of the church. To do so is to deny the relation of the individual to the corporate Christian fellowship. This relation may be more or less clearly defined in a particular instance, but it is there just by virtue of the couple's approaching a minister and not a justice of the peace. From both the study of Calvin and the case histories, the presence of the corporate decision is seen to be a condition of remarriage. This decision is expressed by an interpretation of the law — usually through the minister, or by corporate decision on the part of the presbytery, bishop's council, or ruling equivalent.

The final condition of remarriage is that the marriage must be " *in the Lord.*" This phrase can be variously interpreted by various people. In Calvin's view, as well as in view of the dynamics of remarriage, there are certain things which this phrase must mean.

To be married " in the Lord " means to maintain a tension between the second and third conditions — i.e., a tension between the individual and the corporate dimensions. Such marriage is a call of God. It recognizes that the decision for remarriage does not lie in the hands of one man. Just as surely, the individual cannot escape a vital part in making the ultimate decision. To forget the responsibility of the individual is to abdicate one's real identity as an individual in the presence of the mass. This is almost to say that one needs to recognize the reality of himself just as much as the reality of God. To deny it is dangerous for remarriage.

To recognize the place of only the individual, however, is to make a god of the individual. When this happens, not only the fact of God is missed, but also the fact of dynamics in human living is forgotten. To make a god of the individual destroys the interpersonalness of all personal relations and results in a crystallization of those relationships. This is what happens with those ministers who categorically say that they will or will not remarry divorced people. Such categorical positions solidify all relationships, so that the interpersonal aspect is not allowed to function.

To be married " in the Lord," likewise means that one must not be tied to the past or blind to the present. To be bound to the past is, Biblically speaking, idolatry. From the standpoint of human dynamics, such idolatry grows out of a sense of guilt or a lack of security. The minister or couple who are bound to the past are not free to be themselves in the present. In a sense, they are not free to marry in the Lord because the past is their lord. To be blind to the present, and not dynamically related to the present, is the result of preoccupation either with the past, with one's sense of guilt, or with one's fears.

Therefore, when two people wish to remarry, they must be aware that the past is in the past, there must be a coming to terms with the basis of being or existence in the present, and the future must be seen as related to the present. By seeing the past as in the past, the chains of guilt and danger of idolatry are overcome. Coming to terms with the basis of existence in the present is the dynamic expression of being " in the Lord."

The future is equally important. Throughout his writings, Paul Tillich argues that God is not just an individual being among other individuals. He is being itself. If this is true, then we come to terms with God only in so far as we do it with regard to our past, our present, and our future. Thus, the relationship of the future is important because the desire for future fulfillment, and the drive to a future goal of oneness in marriage, is a part of the present. The rights and place of children, as a part of or a threat to that fulfillment, are also a part of the present. Negatively, this is demonstrated by the persistent question in the minds of those who have extramarital relations, " What if I get pregnant? " Even for married people, the fear of pregnancy is often an influential part of the present dynamic. Just as real in the lives of some people, but often unheralded, is the hope of pregnancy. "We want to get married because we want to have children " was the response of one couple who came from a rather Bohemian background. For this reason, the Bible and the laws of the church have always seen the place of children as having the right to be " well born."

This concept of being married " in the Lord " means that there is one considered, ultimate authority in the decision to remarry. That is the authority that comes *not* from the minister or from the law of the church or land, nor from the desires of the couple. It is the authority of a revelation that breaks through the counseling situation into the presence of the parties concerned. I have defined it as the point of " readiness for marriage."

The presence of this authority is recognized both by Calvin and by modern psychotherapy. In Calvin, it is seen in his attitude toward an " imprudent marriage," wherein he counseled that a couple should be held as a part of the church not only in order that they might not go off to have an even worse effect on the lives of others but also in order that something might reach them. It is seen again in many counseling cases where the counselee sometimes even speaks of the event as being suddenly a revelation.

The dynamic approach to the interpretation of " in the Lord " means that the marriage in itself must be in the line of creative acts. If the past is to be in the past, it must be recognized that each present moment immediately becomes a past. Each minute immediately moves into the past and each new " present moment" must come to terms with it. Because this " old present moment " is something new in the presence of each succeeding experience, every " now " is an entirely *new creation*. Each new moment must create itself in a relationship of awareness to the entire past.

Sometimes this is very mild. We do it every living moment. There is nothing very soul-shaking about adjusting to that part of my past which involved typing the previous line. At times, however, this can shake a person to his roots. One girl came to talk about getting married. She was in love with a divorced man. She had a very good interview and left with a feeling of appreciation for some of the concerns she had been able to work through. A week later, she called upon the minister in near-hysterics.

She had just discovered that all the time this man had been courting her, he had been engaged to marry another woman, and, in fact, was to marry the other woman that next week. Coming to terms with the present experience of his phone call, which now was a part of her past, meant a total rearrangement of her understanding of the past. The beautiful memories suddenly took on a cynical color, and each separate memory had to be dealt with. Each new moment is a new creation.

We must now make a diversion. The concept of the *new creation*, to be understood properly in this context, must be seen in the framework of Calvin. Because the present Presbyterian law, even in the statement of the Confession of Faith, seems to miss this concept, the subject could not be discussed in comparing the position of Calvin and the law. Further, in view of the fact that the scope of his view of creation is not explicitly spelled out, but only discovered by looking back at the way Calvin dealt with it, the Reformer's view of creation becomes a part of this constructive interpretation of his contribution to the remarriage of divorced persons.

Someone may observe that much of what has been said seems in no way different from what could be said with regard to a first marriage. This is quite correct. There are parallels. The difference comes in this area of the new creation. With a remarriage, the " stuff " out of which the new creation comes is different from that of a first marriage simply because there has not yet been the death of a " one flesh " relationship. This is a difference, not just in the type of experience, but in the quality of the experience.

From all that has been said, the place of forgiveness in remarriage emerges as central. It must have a real place in the law of each particular denomination. It must have a real place in the application of that law by either the minister, the officers of a given church, or the officials of a denomination.

The argument of the second chapter and the basis of my position could be summarized by saying that forgiveness is the ingredient that makes a person ready for marriage. Everyone shares in the guilt of any marriage failure. The church, the culture, the "other woman," are as much to blame as the individual himself. There is no such thing as innocency. Without forgiveness, there can be no means of freedom from guilt. Forgiveness is the means by which all the non-innocents put the past in the past. Forgiveness is the potential for freedom and fulfillment in the future.

In face-to-face conversation, this means that each forgives the other and accepts what the other brings to the new marriage. The experience of the minister with Dorie, wherein she accepted him so that he relaxed and became a better minister, shows how this applies even to the clergy. In the depth of personal emotions, each person must forgive himself. In the history of a person's experience, each one must forgive those who are in the past.

In the Christian view of time, forgiveness means, ultimately, accepting the forgiveness of God. The fact is that society may not forgive. The divorced spouse, the parents, and the relatives may make the individual *persona non grata*. Yet it is possible for a person to feel forgiven by God. The acceptance of forgiveness on the part of the minister, the fiancé, the church, and the culture is the means by which one makes real the acceptance of God's forgiveness.

It is here that the life and death of Christ become important. The cross is the event in human history in which the forgiveness of God has been made real. Christ is the new creation. Through the experience of coming to a moment of remarriage, the Christian faith becomes an actual experience and not just an intellectual belief. It is the way in which Jesus Christ becomes experienced by the couple.

The minister, too, is involved in this. Nothing can save him from the ultimate arbitrariness of making a decision. The authority and basis for this decision, however, cannot be his conscience. Rather, the basis is the experience of God's forgiveness in Christ becoming real in the relationship between the minister and the couple.

A suggested law that would allow for this all-important point would read as follows:

> Inasmuch as the church must uphold the Christian home and the permanence of the marriage tie, and at the same time minister sympathetically to any who have failed in this holy relation, ministers who are requested to remarry divorced persons shall ascertain whether there is penitence for past sin and failure, realization of total and present forgiveness, and intention to enter, with the help of God, and through his church, into a marriage of love, honor, forbearance, and loyalty, which will continue as long as both shall live. To implement the guidance of the church in the remarriage of divorced persons, and to protect against any marriages that are not in the Lord, a minister shall officiate at the marriage of a divorced person only after such period of time as is necessary to be ready for the new creation of one flesh, only after he and the couple feel guided by the Holy Spirit to that marriage, and only upon interpreting the Scripture and the law of the church under the dynamic guidance of that Holy Spirit.
>
> Every concern of remarriage shall be subject to the review of _____. Every couple denied remarriage by a given minister shall have recourse to a committee

of _____ and shall be so informed. Any decision of
_____ shall be final subject to the normal rules of
appeal.

The framework for this particular statement comes
from the Presbyterian law. It thus serves as an example
of the way in which any church law can be reworked in
order to recognize the real questions that are involved
in the remarriage of divorced persons. The blank spaces in
this statement would be filled in on the basis of the
church government involved. For a Presbyterian, the
word "presbytery" would be inserted. For a Congregationalist, the phrase "board of trustees" would probably
be used. For an Episcopalian, the reference would, of
course, be to the bishop.

The first sentence of this statement recognizes the corporate nature of the marriage relationship. It sees the future as related to the present. It understands the need for
awareness of the past and the necessity of forgiveness for
it. The sentence comprehends the reality of fulfillment as
one flesh. The second statement implements the concept
of corporateness by recognizing the corporate relationship
of both the couple and the minister, and the three — not
just the minister — in regard to the denomination. Finally,
the statement is aware of the Christian view of time that
was considered fundamentally essential to the proper approach to the remarriage of divorced persons.

As he is approached by a couple for marriage, what,
then, is the minister's role in the application of this law?
What is the place of the church officer?

Fundamentally, whether officer or minister, his task is
to set up the structure and the conditions whereby God
can work in the situation and forgiveness can be realized.
This structure includes the denomination's position, the

attitude of the particular church in question, and the approach of the individual minister. This means that:

1. The minister, operating in this structure, must then be accepting. It is by accepting the couples as they are that he demonstrates forgiveness. In so doing, the minister creates the type of situation in which the Holy Spirit can work and whereby there can come about the new creation.

2. The minister must deal with the initial uneasiness. He can do this by accepting and understanding even this emotion. One girl began an interview by saying, " Well, I'm ready for the cross-examination." The minister replied, " You feel I'm really going to put you through it? " This immediately opened a discussion of the girl's feelings about what was going on right then and her attitude to the whole approach to marriage. By doing this, the minister allowed her to deal with the surface issues. As she gained confidence, she then began to work through to the deeper problems.

3. The minister and the church officer must see and accept the sense of personal failure. This means that the ways must be recognized in which failure sometimes expresses itself. Some persons feel deep guilt and outwardly manifest their sense of failure. Others are very defensive. This defensiveness is the way in which the failure is expressed. Still others are almost schizophrenic about it. The failure is in " another world " that they do not recognize. If so, the minister must see this and help the couple to see it.

4. The minister must look for a sense of realized forgiveness. Lack of this is evidence that the person is still tied to the past, that the previous marriage is not dead, and that the person is not, therefore, free to remarry.

5. The officers of the church must take seriously their part in making possible the awareness of this forgiveness. In a way that is within the context of their particular church, they must discern what procedures can make this possible. Otherwise, the minister's decision becomes just individualistic. Moreover, the couple is deprived of the opportunity to experience forgiveness in its fullest.

6. Both church officers and the minister must allow for expression of fulfillment. This experience cannot be brought about. It just comes. The minister helps prepare for it. The officers help provide for its experience. The marriage ceremony allows for the outward expression of confession, prayer, and Christian fulfillment. The real experience, however, may occur at times other than during the ceremony. Those responsible must help the couple prepare for it.

7. In the event that a pastor does not feel the *kairos* of Christian fulfillment, the reality of forgiveness, the sense of penitence, and all that makes for "readiness to marry," he must deny the marriage for himself alone. To say that these facts could not be experienced in the presence of one minister does not say that they could not be experienced in the presence of another. To argue otherwise is to make the minister a god. Therefore, I would hold that restrictions of marriage that are based on comity are to be rejected.

This position is consistent with the Scripture, with the position of the Reformation period, and with the insights of modern pastoral care. To realize forgiveness in the corporate and individual areas of life is to achieve integrity in one's relation to God. To help achieve this relationship in the experience of marriage is the purpose of the marriage law. I am convinced that mine is not the last word on the subject. I am equally convinced that first words on the subject have been tragically few. In the hope that it will provoke more thought, more action, and more experience in the relevancy of the Christian faith, this approach to remarriage is presented.[93]

≪≫

EPILOGUE

If the reader of this book feels only that he has been helped in understanding the question of remarriage, I will be grateful but not successful. There are many implications of the preceding pages that must be recognized by every Christian.

In the preface to a book on marriage published by the Presbyterian Church in 1932, the editor said:

> We clergymen are justly criticized that we have spent much of our time in other than the sane, scientific, and healthful teaching of our young people on the subject. We have not been either willing or skilled in the treatment of poorly adjusted lives. . . . The silence of the clergy on these important themes is one of the ominous signs in all this horrible catastrophe which has overtaken us.[94]

These words remain true today, and they apply to church members as well as ministers.

The focus of the problem in this study is but one of the many problems that men and women face. These problems will not be solved by reading a book. These are problems of human relationship — relationship to other humans and to God. If they could be solved by reading

literature, then church secretaries to handle mailing
would be the answer to our ills. On the contrary, there
are four implications of this — and every relevant book on
human lives — that must be taken seriously. These implications should be in the foreground of every Christian
whether he is in a pew, a pulpit, a denominational judica-
tory, or a church council.

1. There is a pastoral theology that must be taken seriously. The time has passed when matters of human relationship can be seen as just questions of technique on the one
hand, or a last chapter to "basic principles" on the other.
Almost four hundred years ago, a pastor observed that the
insights of the Reformation would never be realized until
the church developed a real pastoral theology. It never
has; and its fumbling in the presence of something like
remarriage is but one consequence.

2. The doctrine of the Holy Spirit can and must be approached. Many have stated that the doctrine of the Holy
Spirit is the most neglected in the church. There have
been some excellent beginnings on recapturing the wonder of this doctrine. None of these, however, actually take
hold at the point where this doctrine really comes alive:
in the experience of the church. Pastoral theology reveals
a proving ground in which the work of the Holy Spirit
ceases to be an abstract principle and becomes a vital
force. In one sense, this book is a study of the way in
which the Spirit works. It is an attempt to get at that
doctrine.

3. Further, this books adds another voice to those already raised about what theology calls "the means of
grace." There is a general movement today toward a re-
evaluation of worship, sacraments, and their use. What is
the meaning of a sacrament, and how does it relate to the

communicant? What do our liturgies really say? Are they expressions of a relevant Christian faith? The marriage liturgy often seems more an expression of an extravagant and pagan culture than of a " one flesh."

4. There are implications here for an approach not so much to church union as to church unity. It was amazing to me that the same basic weaknesses and the same basic needs were found in all the church laws. Serious attention to the area of realized forgiveness could bring all church laws on remarriage into a basic unity — even though it would be expressed in different words.

We believe that God was incarnate in Christ. We also believe that the church is the body of Christ. When we are afraid to look at the church in relation to remarriage, to segregation, to economic problems, it means that we are afraid to look at Christ where he is.

The over-all implication of this book is that we have not merely a basis for a pastoral theology or a theology of the Holy Spirit or a view of the means of grace; the over-all implication is that the church need not be a ghetto — in Heim's word. Rather, the churches of today have the means for a basic theology that is unifying because it is related to the real questions that are being asked of it. In short, the witness of this book is not only to a Christian solution for the question of remarriage but also to the fact that there can be an ecumenical theology. The witness is to the fact that the " church can be the church," which brings the answer rather than another part of the problem. If these words have had any merit, then let us be obedient to this witness. Let church marriages again be Christian marriages!

《》

NOTES

1. Karl Heim, *Christian Faith and Natural Science,* tr. by N. Horton Smith (Harper & Brothers, 1957), p. 28.

2. Mary Baker Eddy, *Science and Health* (Trustees Under the Will of Mary Baker G. Eddy, 1875), p. 57.

3. *Ibid.,* p. 60.

4. James G. Emerson, Jr., "The Remarriage of Divorced Persons in The United Presbyterian Church U.S.A.," pp. 48 ff. Unpublished Ph.D dissertation. University of Chicago, 1959.

5. John Calvin, *Institutes of the Christian Religion,* tr. by John Allen (Presbyterian Board of Christian Education, Philadelphia), IV. viii. 5.

6. Seward Hiltner, *Preface to Pastoral Theology* (Abingdon Press. 1958).

7. Because of this fact, I am of the opinion that the term "pastoral theology" should include more than what Dr. Hiltner describes as the "shepherding function" of the minister. It should apply to the minister's total operation.

8. Benjamin N. Cardozo, *The Nature of the Judicial Process* (Yale University Press, 1921), p. 28.

9. Roscoe Pound, *An Interpretation of the Philosophy of Law* (Yale University Press, 1922), pp. 60, 99.

10. John Calvin, *Letters,* tr. by David Constable and ed. by J. Bonnett (Constable & Co., Ltd., Edinburgh, 1855), II, p. 200.

11. John T. McNeill, *The History and Character of Calvinism* (Oxford University Press, 1954), p. 138.

12. John Donne, *Devotions,* XVII.

13. Joannis Calvin, *Opera Selecta,* ed. by Petrus Barth and Guilelmus Niesel, (Monachii in Aedibus Chr. Kaiser, 1952), II, p. 346. For this and the following translations, I am indebted to the help of Mr. Wiebe Glastra, of Holland, and to Dr. Severn Mantel, an authority on international law who formerly lived in Austria. Both men spent considerable time in going over the French texts with me. For the final translations, particularly where there may have been some disagreement over the words, I am responsible.

14. *Ibid.*

15. *Ibid.,* p. 347.

16. *Ibid.*

17. *Ibid.,* p. 348.

18. *Ibid.*

19. *Ibid.*

20. *Ibid.,* p. 349.

21. *Ibid.*

22. *Ibid.,* p. 351.

23. *Ibid.*

24. *Ibid.*

25. *Ibid.,* p. 353.

26. *Ibid.,* p. 354.

27. *Ibid.,* p. 355.

28. Georgia Harkness, *John Calvin: The Man and His Ethics* (Henry Holt & Co., Inc., 1931), p. 151.

29. William Cole, *Sex in Christianity and Psychotherapy* (Oxford University Press, 1955), p. 130.

30. Harkness, *op. cit.,* p. 151.

31. *Ibid.,* p. 152.

32. Calvin, *Letters,* I, p. 161.

33. John Calvin, *Instruction in Faith,* tr. by Paul T. Fuhrmann (The Westminster Press, 1949), p. 42.

34. *Ibid.,* p. 33.

35. Ibid., p. 25.

36. Calvin, *Institutes,* II. viii. 6.

37. *Ibid.,* II. viii. 7.

38. John Calvin, *Questions and Answers Upon the Duties of the Christian Religion* (Trustees of the Publishing Fund, 1823), p. 50.

39. *Ibid.*, p. 51.

40. John Calvin, *Commentary on a Harmony of the Evangelists Matthew, Mark, and Luke,* tr. by William Pringle (Wm. B. Eerdmans Publishing Company, 1949), II, p. 380.

41. *Ibid.*, p. 293.

42. John Calvin, *Commentaries on the Four Last Books of Moses,* tr. by C. W. Bingham (Wm. B. Eerdmans Publishing Company, 1950), p.187.

43. Calvin, *Institutes,* II. iv. 7.

44. *Ibid.*, III. iii. 2.

45. For further evidence of this point, I would call attention to the discussion of "time" and also of Calvin in my dissertation (see note 4).

46. Harkness, *op. cit.*, p. 35.

47. John Calvin, *Commentaries on the Epistles of Paul to Galatians and Ephesians,* tr. by William Pringle (Wm. B. Eerdmans Publishing Company, 1948), p. 322.

48. *Ibid.*, p. 323.

49. Calvin, *Institutes,* III. iv. 13.

50. *Ibid.*

51. *Ibid.*, III. iii. 3.

52. *Ibid.*

53. Gibson Winter, quoting Luther in an unpublished paper for the Office of Family Education Research of the Board of Christian Education of The United Presbyterian Church in the U.S.A.

54. Hugh C. Warner, *Divorce and Remarriage* (George Allen & Unwin, Ltd., London, 1954), p. 45.

55. *Ibid.*, p. 53.

56. Oscar B. Maurer, *Manual of the Congregational Christian Churches* (The Pilgrim Press, 1947), p. 65.

57. *Ibid.*, p. 68.

58. *Constitution and Canons for the Government of the Protestant Episcopal Church in the United States of America.* Adopted in General Conventions 1789–1958 (printed for the Convention, 1958), pp. 44 ff. and 47. Edwin Augustine White and Jackson A. Dykman, *Annotated Constitution and Canons for the Government of the Protestant Episcopal Church in the United States of America.* I. Adopted in General Conventions

1789–1952 (The Seabury Press, Inc., 1954), pp. 354 ff. Used by permission.

59. White and Dykman, *op. cit.*, p. 357.

60. *Ibid.*

61. *Ibid.*, p. 359.

62. *Ibid.*, pp. 361 ff.

63. *Ibid.*, p. 370.

64. *Ibid.*

65. *Discipline of The Methodist Church,* ed. by Bishop Nolan B. Harmon (The Methodist Publishing House, 1957), p. 130.

66. *Supra,* Chapter IV.

67. *Christian Guidance on Marriage and Family Life* (The Board of Social Missions of the United Lutheran Church in America, New York, 1956). Used by permission.

68. " Report of the Committee on Social and Moral Welfare: Divorce for Desertion," *Minutes of the Seventh Biennial Convention of the United Lutheran Church in America,* New York, 1930. Used by permission.

69. *Ibid.*

70. *Ibid.*

71. *The Constitution of The United Presbyterian Church in the United States of America,* Confession of Faith, Chapter XXIV. (The Office of the General Assembly of The United Presbyterian Church in the U.S.A., 1960.)

72. *Ibid.*, Directory for Worship, Chapter XIV, Sections 5 and 7.

73. *Ibid.*, Sections 10 and 11.

74. Leonard J. Trinterud, *The Forming of an American Tradition* (The Westminster Press, 1949), p. 76.

75. *The Presbyterian Digest* (Presbyterian Church in the U.S.A., 1898), p. 96.

76. *Ibid.*, p. 97.

77. *Ibid.*

78. *Ibid.*, p. 99.

79. *Ibid.*, p. 94.

80. *Minutes of the General Assembly* (Presbyterian Church in the U.S.A., 1928), pp. 60–61.

81. *Ibid.* (1929), Overture from Presbytery of Dubuque.

82. *Ibid.* (1930), p. 86.

83. *Ibid.*, p. 87.

84. *Ibid.*

85. *Ibid.*, 1950, p. 120.

86. *Ibid.*, p. 121.

87. *Ibid.*, p. 25.

88. Trinterud, *op. cit.*, p. 261.

89. *Ibid.*

90. *The Presbyterian Constitution and Digest* (1956), p. A52.

91. *The Presbyterian Digest* (1898), p. 93.

92. Michigan University School of the Air. Broadcast, October 28, 1957.

93. At the General Assembly in 1959 (after the basic manuscript for this book had been written) the Presbyterian Church in the United States (often called the "Southern Presbyterian Church") adopted a new law. This law is excellent. It moves in the direction of the argument of this book. Although there are points where it could be strengthened, and although one senses a slight hesitancy on the corporate dimensions of marriage, I consider this law a major breakthrough in the area of church polity and ecclesiastical standards.

94. By Dr. Ralph Marshall Davis, in *Twenty-four Views of Marriage*, p. xiii. (Presbyterian Church in the U.S.A., 1932. Issued under the authority of a Commission set up by the General Assembly.)

INDEX

Adultery, 23 ff., 38, 42, 75, 88 ff., 94, 97 ff., 114 ff., 122, 132 ff., 147

Anxiety, 60

Bible, 19, 33, 42 ff.
  Matthew, 46, 126
  Corinthians, 126–127
  Deuteronomy, 44
  Malachi, 45
  Hillel, 44
  Jesus, 45–48
  Paul, 45–48
  Shammai, 43

Calvin, 23–24, 42, 52, 84 ff.
Calvinists, 51–52
Causes of divorce, 13
Children, 72 ff.
Christian Science, 35
Church, 15, 68. *See also* Corporateness; Denominations
Communications, 62–65 ff.
Communion, 22, 154 ff.

Confession, 22
Corporateness, 84 ff., 101 ff., 137 ff., 170 ff.
Counseling, nondirective, 153 ff., 169
Cross of Christ, the, 174 ff.
Culture, 42, 67 ff., 75–77, 142 ff.

Death, 42, 46–47, 53, 58
Deism, 143
Denominations, 67
  Baptist, 15
  Congregationalist, 15, 109–110
  Episcopalian, 15, 109, 111–119
  Lutheran, 15, 121–126
  Methodist, 15, 109, 119–120
  Orthodox, 15
  Presbyterian, 15, 109, 126 ff.
  Roman Catholic, 15, 18
  Society of Friends, 15
Desertion, 20, 89 ff., 94, 122, 132, 134, 136
Divorce, 19. *See also* Laws

Ecumenical movement, 182

Faith, 73, 77–80
Fear, 73
Freedom, 70–71
Fulfillment. *See* Time: *kairos*

Guilt, 22 ff., 54, 71, 74 ff., 104, 120, 137, 174, 177

Holy Spirit, 150–156, 177, 181

I-thou, 158
Implication of remarriage issue, 13–15, 182
" In the Lord," 134, 169 ff.
Individualism, 84, 95, 132, 136, 170
Infidelity, 143
Innocence, 20, 38, 99, 118, 120, 134

John Knox, 85

Laws, inadequate, 14 ff., 49 ff.
    Geneva, 85 ff.
    rewritten, 163, 175
    See also Denominations; Divorce
Legalism, 19, 51, 92, 94
Lord's Supper, 81, 96. *See also* Communion
Luther, 23, 79, 85, 105 ff.

Marriage ceremony, 159 ff.
Minister, a mediator, 25 ff., 67–68, 148 ff., 151
    his procedure, 55 ff., 63 ff., 148 ff.
    a threat, 66
Mormons, 18, 41

New creation, 155, 158 ff., 172 ff.

One flesh, 79, 155, 165
Overconfidence, 72

Pastoral theology, 49, 95, 181
Pietism, 84, 146 ff.

Rapport, 62 ff., 74 ff.
Readiness to marry, 18, 40, 76 ff., 93, 119 ff., 142, 167 ff.
Realized forgiveness, 21 ff., 38, 40, 53 ff., 69, 78 ff., 94, 100, 103 ff., 136, 142, 146, 154 ff., 177 ff.
Revelation, 59, 78 ff.

Self-awareness, 69–74
Sex, 73 ff.
    relations, 155

Time, 34–41, 79–82, 87, 93, 100 ff., 178
    chronos, 36 ff.
    kairos, 40 ff., 80 ff., 101, 137, 178